Editor
Barbara M. Wally, M.S.

Editorial Project Manager
Ina Massler Levin, M.A.

Editor-in-Chief
Sharon Coan, M.S. Ed.

Illustrators
Wendy Chang
Ana Castanares
Agi Palinay

Cover Artists
Jeff Sutherland
Chris Macabitas

Art Coordinator
Denice Adorno

Creative Director
Elayne Roberts

Imaging
Alfred Lau

Product Manager
Phil Garcia

Publishers
Rachelle Cracchiolo, M.S. Ed.
Mary Dupuy Smith, M.S. Ed.

Practice and Learn

Kindergarten

Written and Compiled by

J. L. Smith

Teacher Created Materials, Inc.
6421 Industry Way
Westminster, CA 92683
www.teachercreated.com
©*1999 Teacher Created Materials, Inc.*
Reprinted, 2001
Made in U.S.A.

Table of Contents

Table of Contents (cont.)

Introduction

Practice and Learn is a book that reinforces skills appropriate for a kindergarten student. Both teachers and parents benefit from the variety of pages provided in this book. A parent can use the book to work with his or her child to provide an introduction to new material or practice and reinforce material already familiar to his or her child. Similarly, a teacher can select pages from this book to provide additional practice for concepts taught in the classroom. When tied to what is being covered in class, pages from this book make great homework reinforcement. For ease in finding the appropriate pages, the book is divided into sections by curriculum area.

Language Arts

The language arts section provides a great variety of practice working with letters, sounds, and words. Students have the opportunity to practice the alphabet by playing games with letters, writing letters, and listening for sounds. Students will begin to write words using sounds they hear in words. They also will have the opportunity to begin writing by using the journal prompts. The reading portion of this section provides parents and teachers a plan for working with students on reading skills, while reading much loved nursery rhymes and fairy tales. Students can gain a sense of story telling by reading these time-tested rhymes and tales, as well as develop skills through the follow-up activities provided for each.

Color

By coloring the pages in this section, students can continue to develop their fine motor coordination. Practicing coloring objects an appropriate color is another important component of this section. In addition, students will develop familiarity with color words.

Mathematics

The activities in this section invite students to explore and practice mathematical concepts. Strong emphasis is given to developing number sense. Students will practice counting, grouping objects, and one-to-one correspondence. Other mathematical concepts covered include shapes, patterns, measurement, telling time, and an introduction to addition and subtraction.

Basic Skills

The final section of the book is devoted to helping children practice and develop skills such as tracking, matching and classifying objects, identifying opposites, visual discrimination, sequencing, and a variety of other skills that provide a foundation for future curriculum studies.

Practice and Learn is designed to do exactly what the title says. The pages in this book provide the framework for students to practice and learn kindergarten skills and concepts.

Alphabet-asaurus

Trace the letters on Alphabet-asaurus. Use your best handwriting.

Lots of Letter Legs!

Trace the letters on Ollie Octopus. Use your best handwriting.

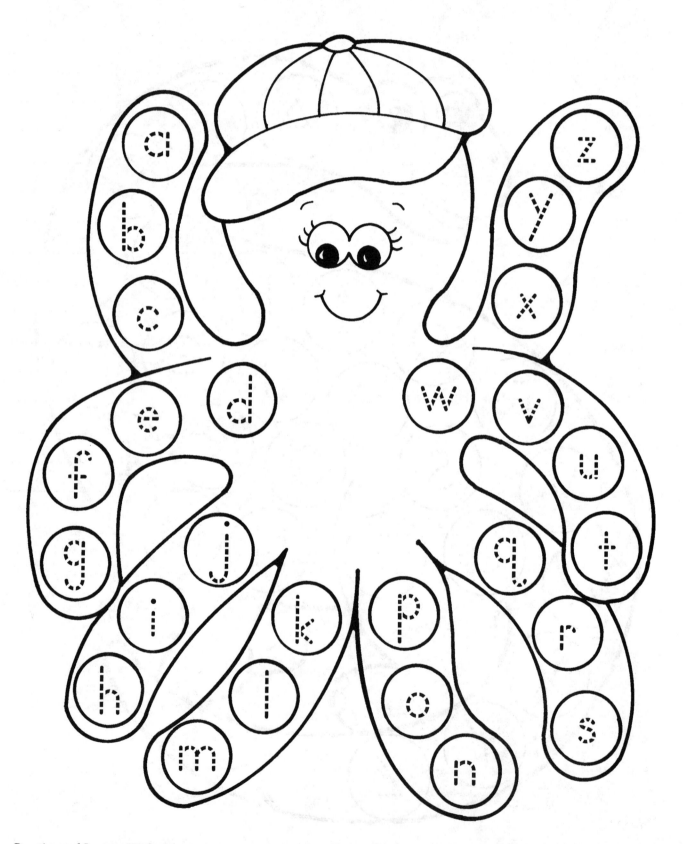

Copy the Uppercase Letters

A ----- B ----- C ----- D -----

E ----- F ----- G ----- H -----

I ----- J ----- K ----- L -----

M ----- N ----- O ----- P -----

Q ----- R ----- S ----- T -----

U ----- V ----- W ----- X -----

Y ----- Z -----

Now I know my ABC's.

Next time won't you sing with me?

Copy the Lowercase Letters

a _____

b _____

c _____

d _____

e _____

f _____

g _____

h _____

i _____

j _____

k _____

l _____

m _____

n _____

o _____

p _____

q _____

r _____

s _____

t _____

u _____

v _____

w _____

x _____

y _____

z _____

Now I know my ABC's.

Tell me, aren't you proud of me?

Alphabet Snake

Fill in the missing uppercase letters on the snake.

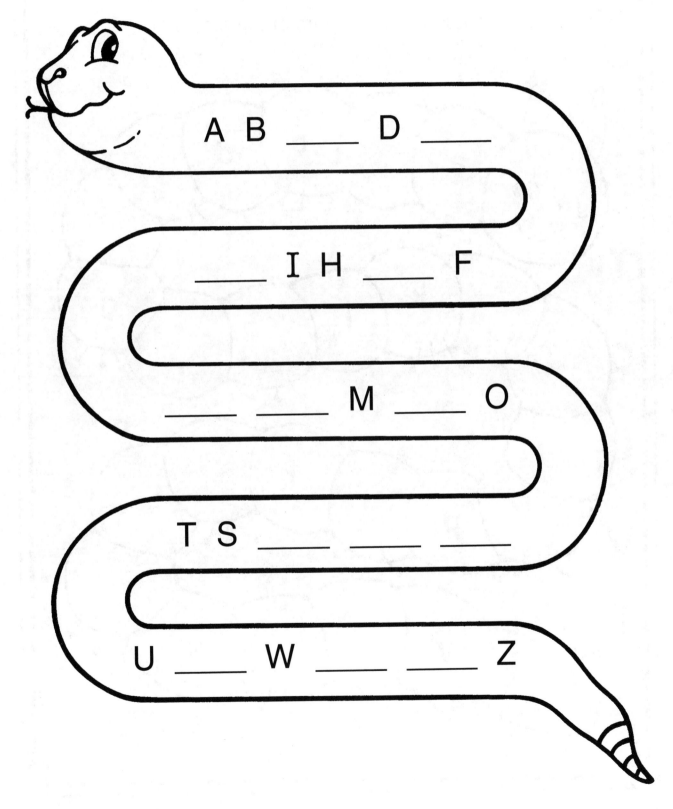

A B ___ D ___

___ I H ___ ___ F

___ ___ ___ M ___ ___ O

T S ___ ___ ___ ___

U ___ W ___ ___ ___ Z

Alpha-Bug

Fill in the missing lowercase letters of the alphabet.

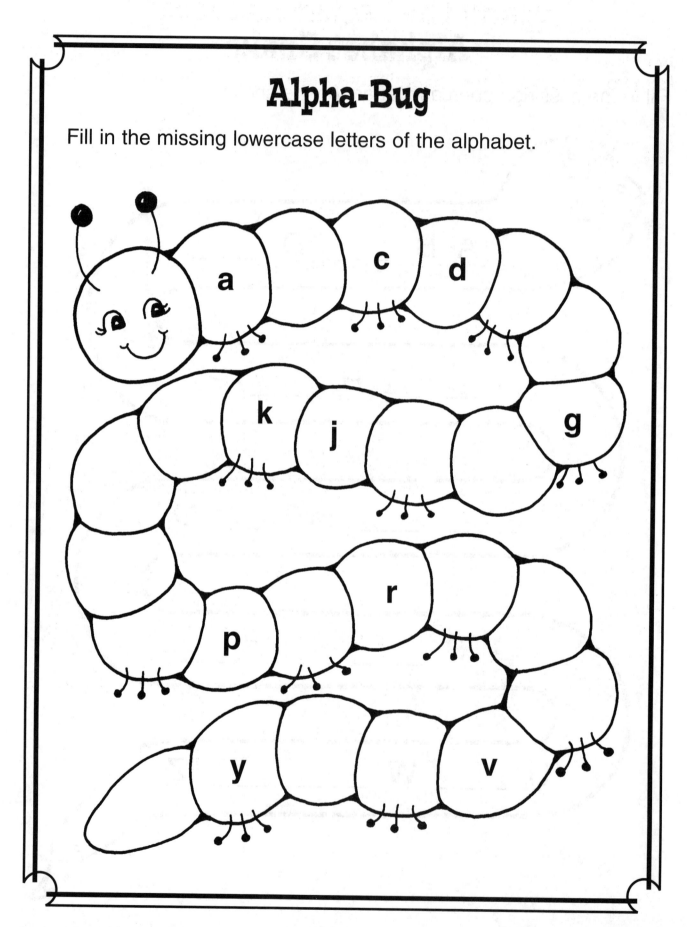

Hang the Letter Laundry

Can you write the missing letters on the laundry? Sing the alphabet to help you discover the missing letters. Color your letter laundry.

A B C D E F G H I J K L M N O P Q R S T U V W X Y Z

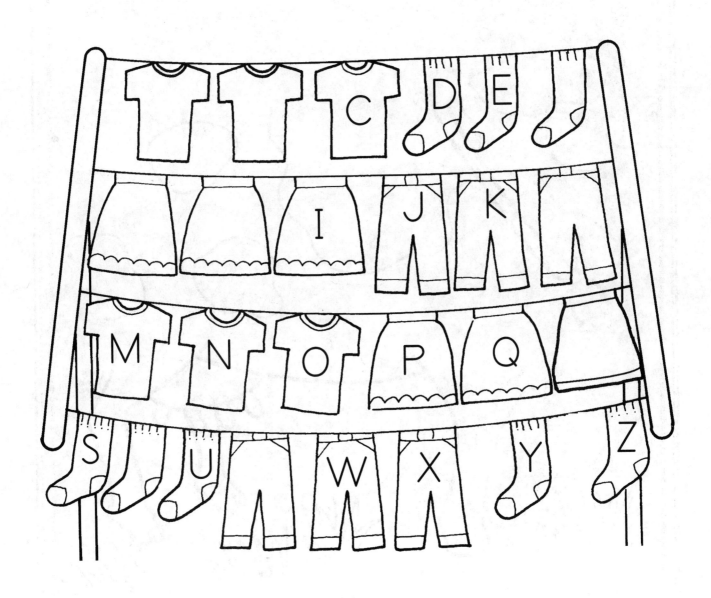

Cow

Draw a line connecting the A-B-C dots. Color the picture.

A Little Cub

1. Connect the dots.

2. Color.

Dot-to-Dot Letter Bear

1. Connect the dots.

2. Color.

Alphabet Maze

Baby Bear is hiding. Help Mama Bear follow the alphabet to find him.

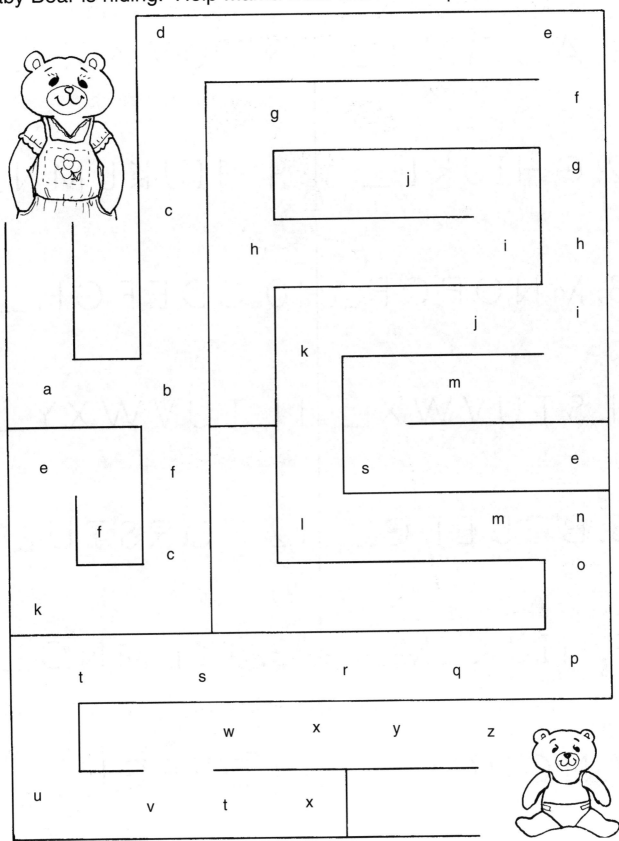

What Comes Next?

Write the next letter in each series.

1. A B C D E F __

2. G H I J K L __

3. M N O P Q R __

4. S T U V W X __

5. B C D E F G __

6. H I J K L M __

7. N O P Q R S __

8. T U V W X Y __

9. H I J K L M N __

10. C D E F G H __

11. T U V W X Y __

12. P Q R S T U __

13. J K L M N O __

14. D E F G H I __

16

Match the Bubbles

Draw lines to match the uppercase letters to the lowercase letters.

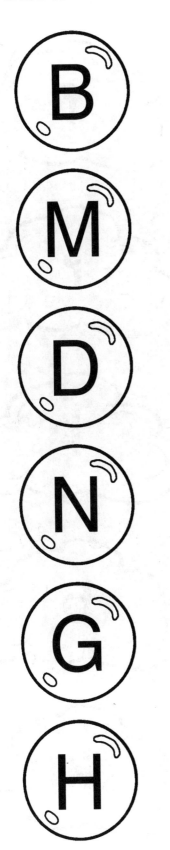

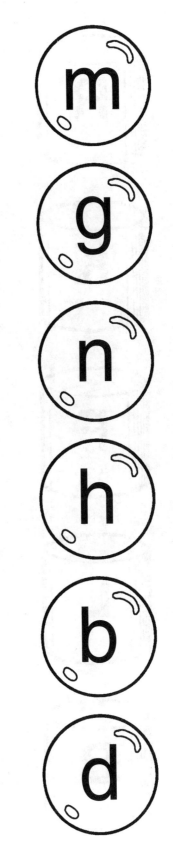

Stack and Puff Match

Draw lines to match the letter partners.

The Letter "A"

Aa

I like to eat apples, as you can see!

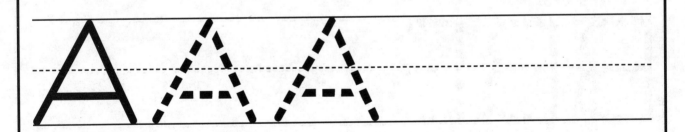

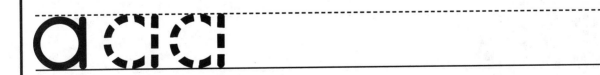

The Letter "B"

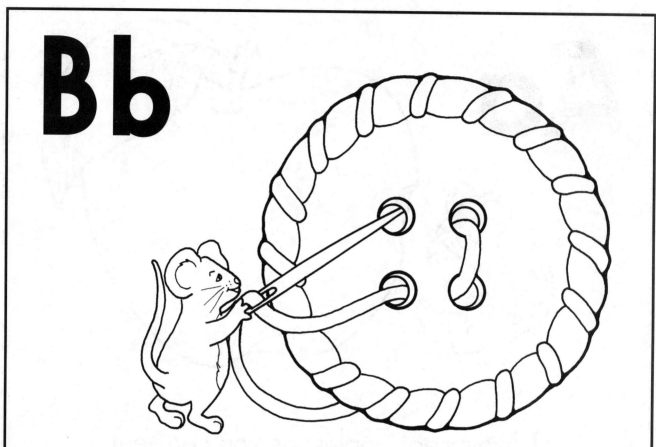

It's a button and I'll sew it on as easy as you please!

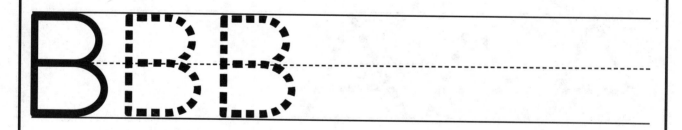

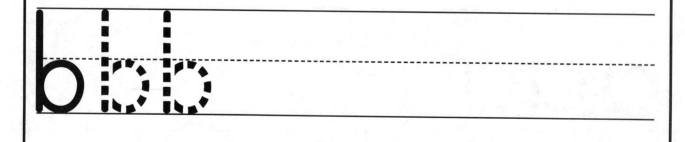

The Letter "C"

Cc

Cookies for dinner taste yummy to me!

Practice and Learn—Kindergarten

The Letter "D"

Dd

Ducky's my friend. He's cute, you'll agree!

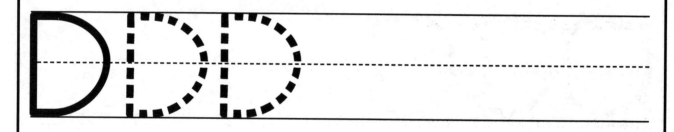

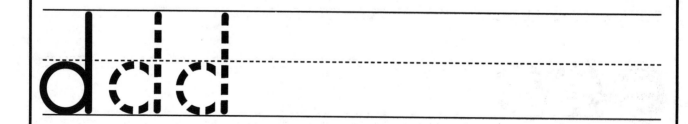

The Letter "E"

"E" is for elephant, a big house guest!

The Letter "F"

F f

"F" is for flowers, pretty as can be.

The Letter "G"

"G" is for a game. Playing is so great!

The Letter "H"

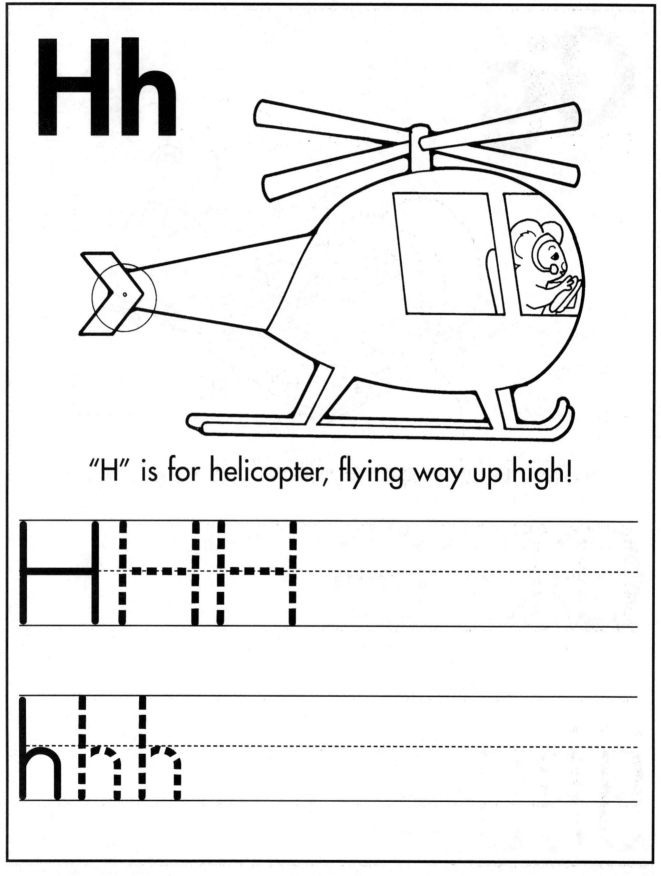

Hh

"H" is for helicopter, flying way up high!

The Letter "I"

Ii

When I talk about myself, "I" is what I say!

The Letter "J"

"J" is for jacks. Have you ever played?

The Letter "K"

Kk

"K" is for kid. You are one, I can tell!

The Letter "L"

"L" is for leprechaun. He is pretend!

The Letter "M"

Mm

"M" is for Mommy, my very best friend!

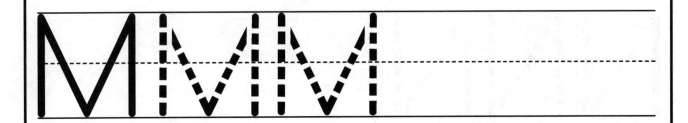

The Letter "N"

N n

"N" is for numbers. Which ones do you know?

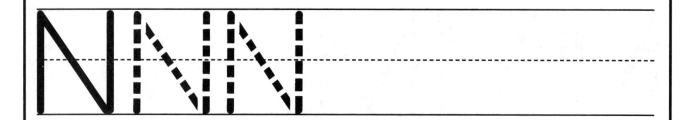

The Letter "O"

"O" is for octopus, my buddy from the sea.

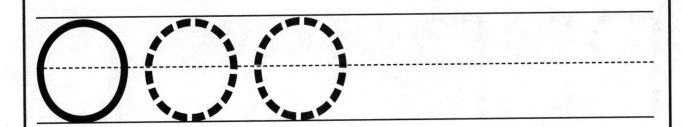

The Letter "P"

"P" is for pie, so tasty, it's true!

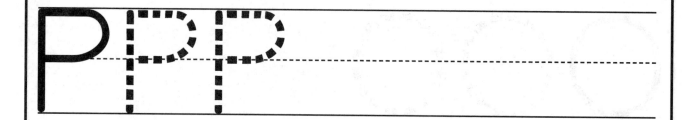

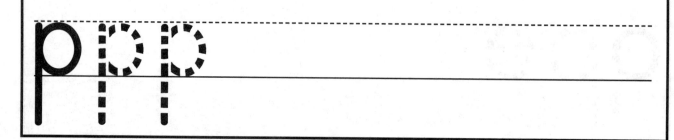

The Letter "Q"

"Q" is for queen in her castle so far!

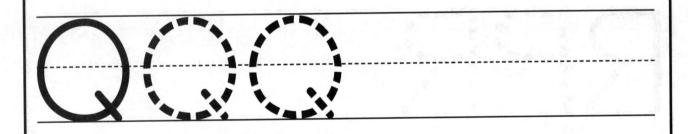

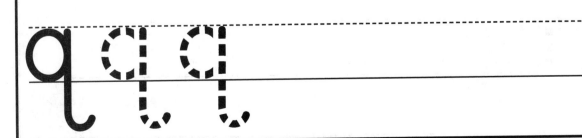

The Letter "R"

"R" is for rabbit. In which hat, can you guess?

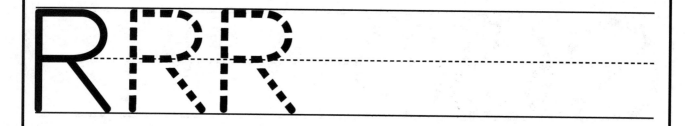

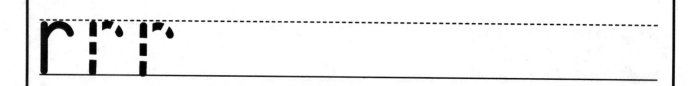

The Letter "S"

Ss

"S" is for snake as harmless as can be!

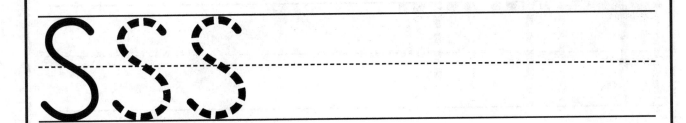

The Letter "T"

"T" is for tail. I have one, do you?

The Letter "U"

U u

"U" is for umbrella. I'm dry as can be!

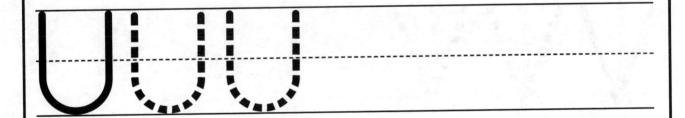

The Letter "V"

"V" is for vacuum. When I clean, I have lots to do!

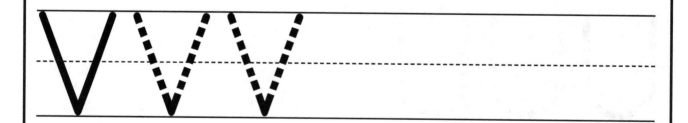

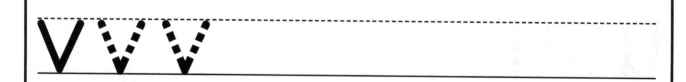

The Letter "W"

"W" is for wagon. Tell me what's next.

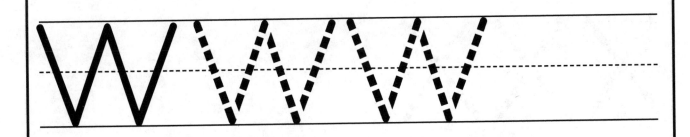

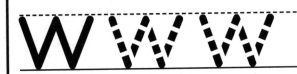

The Letter "X"

"X" is for X-ray. The doctor sees what's inside!

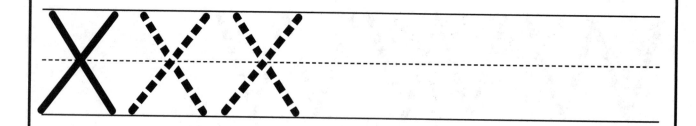

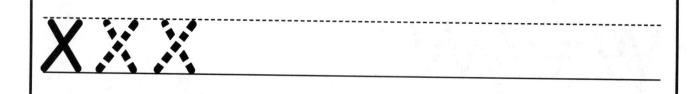

The Letter "Y"

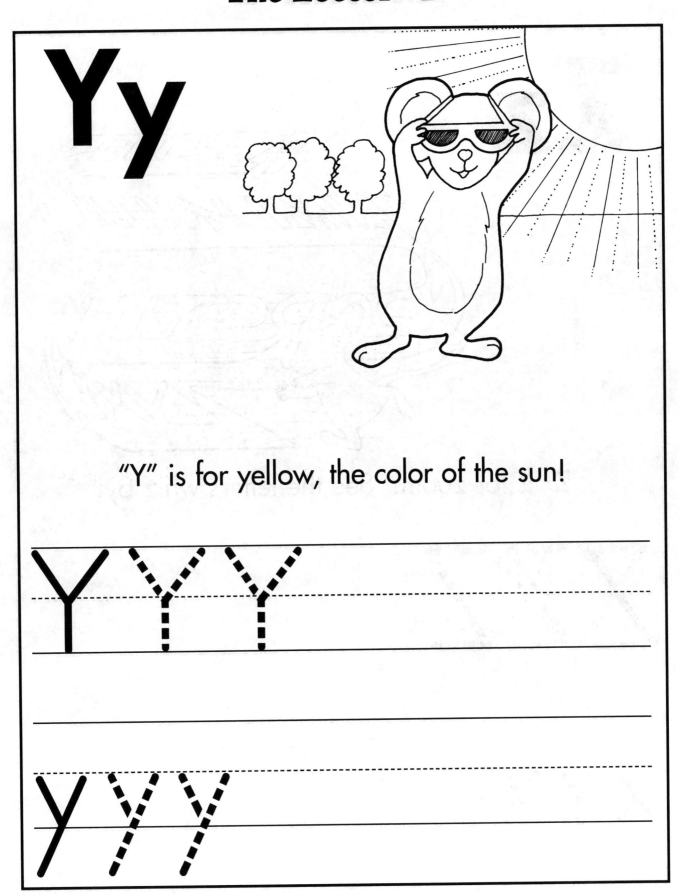

"Y" is for yellow, the color of the sun!

The Letter "Z"

Zz

"Z" is for zoom. See the letters whiz by!

Uppercase

Write the uppercase letter for each lowercase letter.

a _____   b _____   c _____   d _____

e _____   f _____   g _____   h _____

i _____   j _____   k _____   l _____

m _____   n _____   o _____   p _____

q _____   r _____   s _____   t _____

u _____   v _____   w _____   x _____

y _____   z _____

Lowercase

Write the lowercase letter for each uppercase letter.

A_____   B_____   C_____   D_____

E_____   F_____   G _____   H_____

I_____   J_____   K_____   L_____

M_____   N_____   O_____   P_____

Q_____   R_____   S_____   T_____

U_____   V_____   W_____   X_____

Y_____   Z_____

Hidden Reptiles

Color the spaces with dots brown. Color spaces with vowels blue.
Color spaces with consonants green. What reptiles did you find?

Celebrate the Way "A" Sounds

Play this game by finding things that begin with the sounds the letter "A" makes.

1. Say the short "A" sound (as in *ant*) five times. Say the long "A" sound (as in *ape*) five times.

2. Repeat the rhyme:

   The ant and the alligator fishing for an "A"

   Were scared by an ape who chased them both away.

3. Color each thing in the picture that begins with short "A."

Celebrate the Way "B" Sounds

1. Make the letter "B" sound (as in *bear*) five times.

2. Repeat the rhyme:

   The bouncy brown bear, singing a tune,

   Was buzzed by a bee who popped his balloon.

3. How many things that begin with the sound of the letter "B" can you find hidden in the picture? Name everything in the picture. If it begins with the "B" sound, color or circle it.

Celebrate the Way "C" Sounds

Play this game by finding things that begin with the two sounds the letter "C" makes.

1. Say the hard "C" sound (as in *cat*) five times. Say the soft "C" sound (as in *centipede*) five times, too.

2. Repeat the rhyme:

    The cool camel and the fat cat sat

    Watching the centipede swinging his bat!

3. Circle things that start with the same hard "C" sound as camel and cat. Draw a box around the things that start with the same soft "C" sound as in centipede.

Celebrate the Way "D" Sounds

1. Say the "D" sound (as in *duck*) five times.

2. Repeat the rhyme:

   The dolphin, the duck, and the deer

   Draw dinosaur shapes in the mirror.

3. Cut pictures out of old magazines of objects that begin with the "D" sound. Paste them in the box below.

Celebrate the Way "E" Sounds

Be a fisherman! Play this game by fishing for things that begin with the two sounds the letter "E" makes.

1. Make the long "E" sound (as in *eagle*) five times. Make the short "E" sound (as in *elephant*) five times, too.

2. Repeat the rhyme:

   The elephant sat on an eagle

   Eating eggs with his best friend, the beagle!

3. Draw a line from the pictures that begin with long "E" or short "E" to the net. Draw an X through the other pictures.

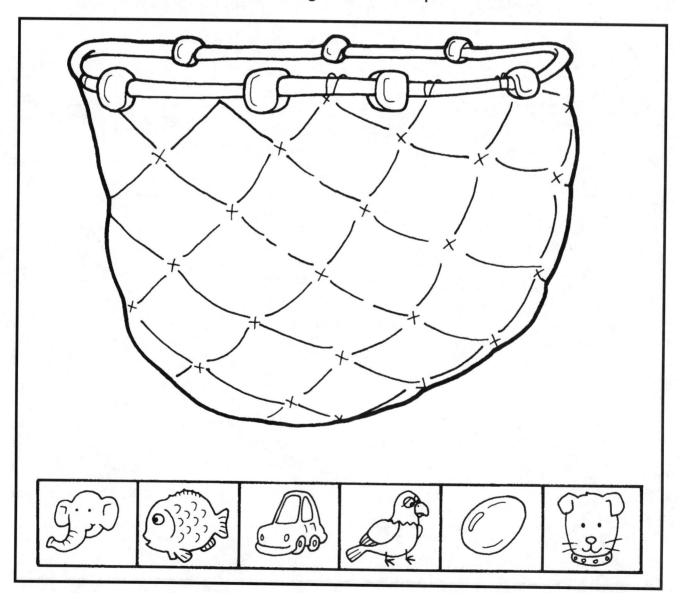

Celebrate the Way "F" Sounds

Play this game by fishing for fish that look alike.

1. Say the "F" sound (as in *fish*) five times.

2. Repeat the rhyme:

> **The fox sings happily**
>
> **At the flamingo jamboree!**

3. Find the matching fish, and color them the same color.

Celebrate the Way "G" Sounds

Play this game by finding things that begin with the two sounds the letter "G" makes.

1. Say the hard "G" sound (as in *gorilla*) five times. Say the soft "G" sound (as in *giraffe*) five times, too.

2. Repeat the rhyme:

    Mr. Gorilla and Mr. Giraffe

    Ate some green grapes and had a good laugh!

3. Color each grape with an uppercase "G" green.

4. Color each grape with a lowercase "g" gray.

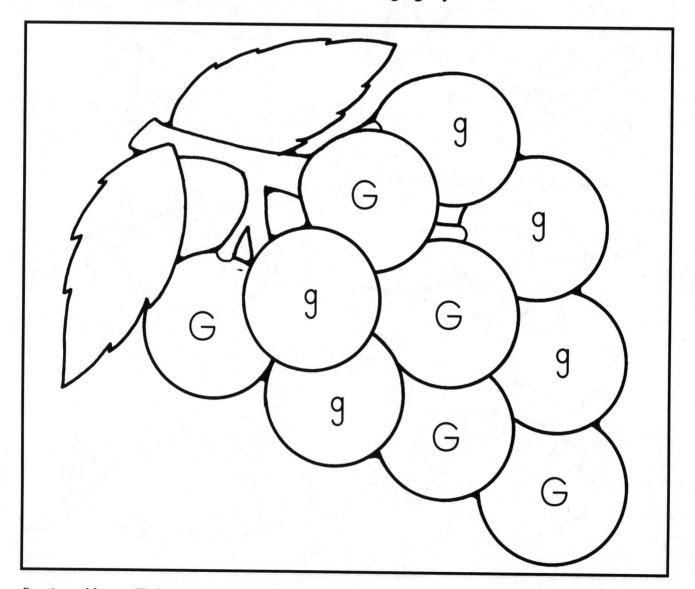

Celebrate the Way "H" Sounds

Play this game by hooking things that begin with the sound the letter "H" makes.

1. Say the "H" sound (as in *house*) five times.

2. Repeat the rhyme:

   The horse and the hippopotamus

   Have a huge happy house that they bought from us.

3. Start fishing for things that start with the "H" sound. Draw a line from fish with "H" pictures to the fish hook. Draw an X through the other fish.

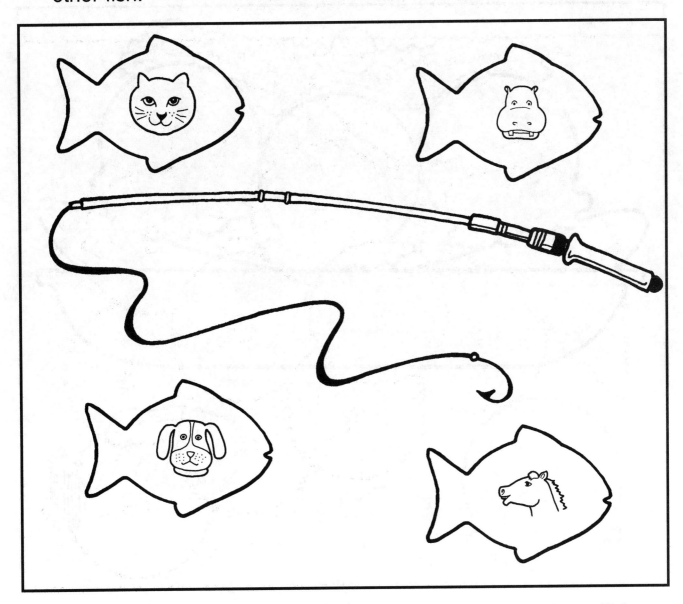

Celebrate the Way "I" Sounds

Make an ice cream sundae.

1. Say the long "I" sound (as in *ice*) five times. Say the short "I" sound (as in *iguana*) five times, too.

2. Repeat the rhyme:

    The iguana licked his ice cream cone

    And talked to insects on the phone!

3. Draw a picture of a word that begins with the "I" sound in each scoop of ice cream.

Celebrate the Way "J" Sounds

Play this game by sorting uppercase and lowercase "J's."

1. Say the "J" sound (as in *jaguar*) five times. Repeat the rhyme:

   The jaguar jumped out of his jacket and boots
   And put on a new jumbo-size jogging suit!

2. Color the jellybeans with uppercase "J" red.

3. Color the jellybeans with lowercase "j" yellow.

4. Color all the other jellybeans different colors.

5. Make the "J" sound each time you color a jellybean.

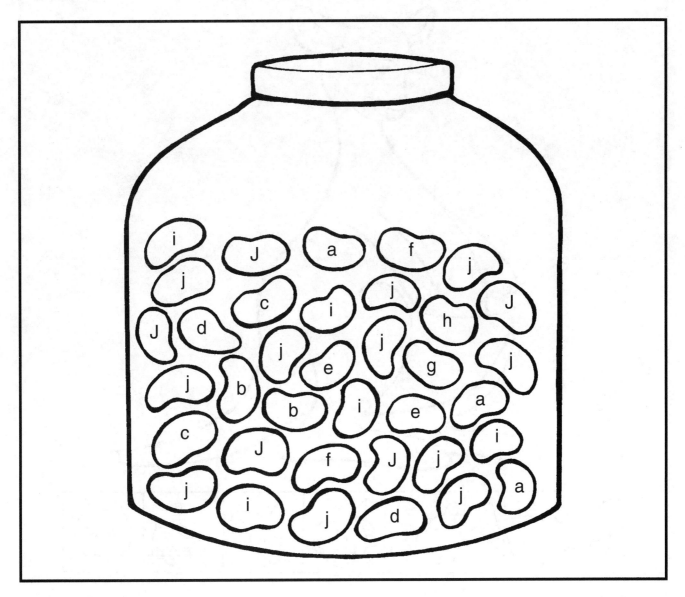

Celebrate the Way "K" Sounds

Play this game by putting things in the kangaroo's pocket that begin with the sound the letter "K" makes.

1. Say the "K" sound (as in *kitten*) five times.

2. Repeat the rhyme:

    The kangaroo king and the kitten queen

    Kissed the koala who acted so mean.

3. If the picture begins with a "K", draw a line to the kangaroo's pouch.

Celebrate the Way "L" Sounds

Play this game by finding things that begin with the sound the letter "L" makes.

1. Say the "L" sound (as in *lion*) five times.

2. Repeat the rhyme:

   The lion, the leopard, and llama were free

   To sit all day long beneath the lollipop tree.

3. Draw a line from the pictures that begin with the sound of "L" to the tree.

Celebrate the Way "M" Sounds

Play this game by finding things that begin with the sound the letter "M" makes.

1. Say the "M" sound (as in *moon*) five times.

2. Repeat the rhyme:

    The monkey, the moose, and the mouse

    Ate macaroni in front of my house!

3. Find pictures of things that start with the same sound as monkey, moose, mouse, and macaroni. Cut and paste them in the moon below.

Celebrate the Way "N" Sounds

Play this game by sorting uppercase and lowercase "N's."

1. Say the "N" sound (as in *nut*) five times.

2. Repeat the rhyme:

   The narwall hid nuts in the nest

   While the newt did his best as a pest!

3. Color purple the nuts with an uppercase "N." Color green the nuts with a lowercase "n." Color the other nuts different colors.

Celebrate the Way "O" Sounds

Play this game by finding things that begin with the sound the letter "O" makes.

1. Say the long "O" sound (as in *oboe*) five times. Say the short "O" sound (as in *octopus*) five times, too.

2. Repeat the rhyme:

   Octopus played his oboe for Owl

   While Orangutan covered his ears with a scowl!

3. Put a circle around things that start with the same sound as octopus, orangutan, and oboe (two different sounds).

Celebrate the Way "P" Sounds

Play this game by finding things that begin with the sound the letter "P" makes.

1. Say the "P" sound (as in *pig*) five times.

2. Repeat the rhyme:

   Mr. Penguin and Mr. Pig

   Sat on a panda and felt so big!

3. Circle all the uppercase and lowercase "P's." Color the picture.

Celebrate the Way "Q" and "R" Sound

Play this game by sorting the uppercase and lowercase "q's" and "r's."

1. Say the "Q" sound (as in *queen*) and the "R" sound (as in *ran*) five times each.

2. Repeat the rhyme:

   The quail quickly ran to the court of the queen.

   The raven and rabbit flew past her unseen.

3. Color the quilt sections with uppercase "Q" red.

   Color the quilt sections with uppercase "R" yellow.

   Color the quilt sections with lowercase "q" purple.

   Color the quilt sections with lowercase "r" pink.

Celebrate the Way "S" Sounds

Play this game by finding things that begin with the sound the letter "S" makes.

1. Say the "S" sound (as in *silly*) five times.

2. Repeat the rhyme:

   The silly squirrel slid down the snake

   Watching seals swim around the lake.

3. Color or circle the things in the picture that begin with the sound the letter "S" makes.

Celebrate the Way "T" Sounds

Play this game by finding the things that begin with the sound the letter "T" makes.

1. Say the "T" sound (as in *turkey*) five times.

2. Repeat the rhyme:

> **The turkey sat on the turtle's back.**
>
> **The tiger chased them around the track!**

3. Cut out things that start with the same sound as turkey and paste them on the train.

Celebrate the Way "U" and "V" Sound

Play this game by sorting "U's" and "V's."

1. Say the long "U" sound (as in *unicorn*) five times. Say the short "U" sound (as in *umbrella*) five times. Next, say the "V" sound (as in *violin*) five times, too.

2. Repeat the rhyme:

   The unicorn's umbrella gave everyone some shade

   While on his violin the vulture played and played.

3. Sort the letters by coloring the "U" sections of the umbrella with purple. Color the sections with "V's" yellow. As you are coloring each section, say the appropriate sound.

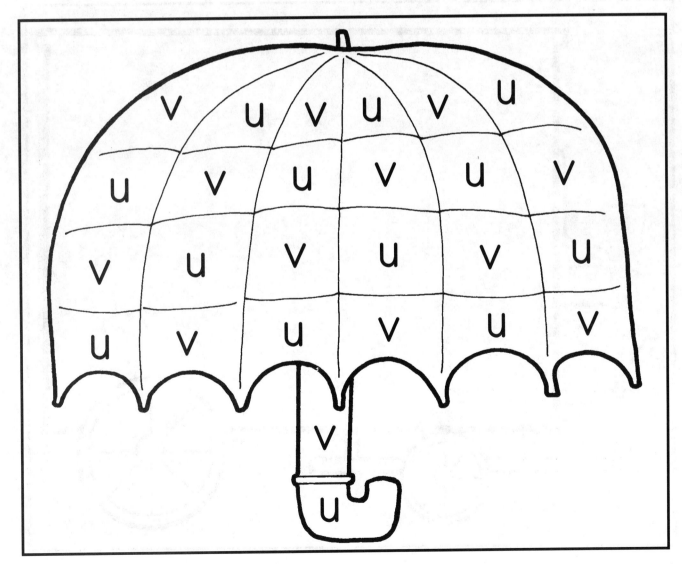

Celebrate the Way "W" Sounds

Play this game by finding things that begin with the sound the letter "W" makes.

1. Say the "W" sound five times.

2. Repeat the rhyme:

   The weasel and the walrus went walking one day

   When a wacky, weird wolf scared them away!

3. Cut out pictures of things that begin with the "w" sound from magazines. Paste them in the wagon below. How full can you get your wagon? After your wagon is full of "W" things, name each thing.

Celebrate the Way "X" and "Y" Sound

Play this game by finding things that begin with the sounds the letters "X" and "Y" make.

1. Say the "X" sound (the two letters "K" and "S" blended together) five times. Say the "Y" sound (as in *yak*) five times, too.

2. Repeat the rhyme:

   The x-ray fish was floating on this back.

   Close by in a yacht, yelled a very loud yak!

3. Put a box around each thing that begins with "Y."

Celebrate the Way "Z" Sounds

Play this game by finding things that begin with the sound the letter "Z" makes.

1. Say the "Z" sound (as in *zig-zag*) five times.

2. Repeat the rhyme:

> **The zebra zig-zagged through the zoo**
> **Looking for me, looking for you!**

3. How many things that begin with "Z" can you find? Circle them.

Missing Letters

- Say each word.
- Listen for the beginning sound.
- Write the missing letter.

1.

_____ nt

2.

_____ ut

3.

_____ ig

4.

_____ an

5.

_____ ing

6.

_____ ow

7.

_____ ish

8.

_____ um

9.

_____ us

More Missing Letters

- Say each word.
- Listen for the beginning sound.
- Write the missing letter.

1.

_____ at

2.

_____ an

3.

_____ ing

4.

_____ tar

5.

_____ og

6.

_____ rog

7.

_____ amp

8.

_____ est

9.

_____ up

Ending Sounds

- Say each word.
- Listen for the ending sound.
- Write the missing letter.

1.

ja_____

2.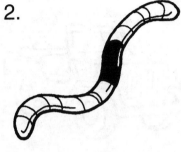

wor _____

3.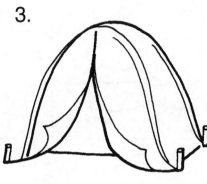

ten _____

4.

han _____

5.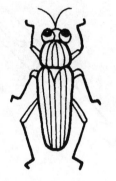

bu _____

6.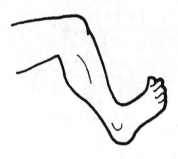

le_____

7.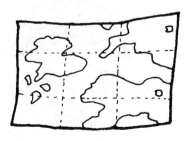

ma _____

8.

su _____

9.

ca _____

More Ending Sounds

- Say each word.
- Listen for the ending sound.
- Write the missing letter.

1.

li _____

2.

jee_____

3.

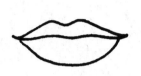

ca _____

4.

in_____

5.

pe _____

6.

a _____

7.

ne _____

8.

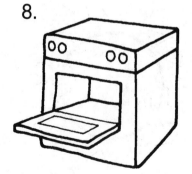

ove _____

9.

we_____

Missing Vowels

- Say each word.
- Listen for the middle sound.
- Write the missing vowel.

1.

p ___ g

2.

d ___ g

3.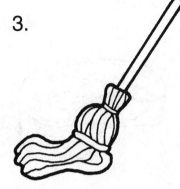

m ___ p

4.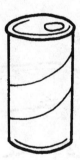

c ___ n

5.

j ___ t

6.

s ___ n

7.

b ___ g

8.

w ___ g

9.

r ___ t

Practice and Learn—Kindergarten

More Missing Vowels

- Say each word.
- Listen for the middle sound.
- Write the missing vowel.

1.

h ____ m

2.

b ____ d

3.

t ____ n

4.

d ____ g

5.

s ____ t

6.

t ____ b

7.

r ____ g

8.

b ____ s

9.

m ____ p

Sound It Out

- Look at each picture.
- Say the word.
- Write the sounds you hear.

1.

___ ___ ___

2.

___ ___ ___

3.

___ ___ ___

4.

___ ___ ___

5.

___ ___ ___

6.

___ ___ ___

7.

___ ___ ___ ___

8.
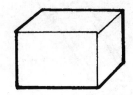

___ ___ ___ ___

9.

___ ___ ___ ___

More Sound It Out

- Look at each picture.
- Say the word.
- Write the sounds you hear.

1.

_____ _____ _____

2.

_____ _____ _____

3.

_____ _____ _____

4.

_____ _____ _____

5.

_____ _____ _____

6.

_____ _____ _____

7.

_____ _____ _____

8.

_____ _____ _____

9.

_____ _____ _____

Match and Rhyme

1. Draw a line to the rhyming picture.

2. Color the pictures.

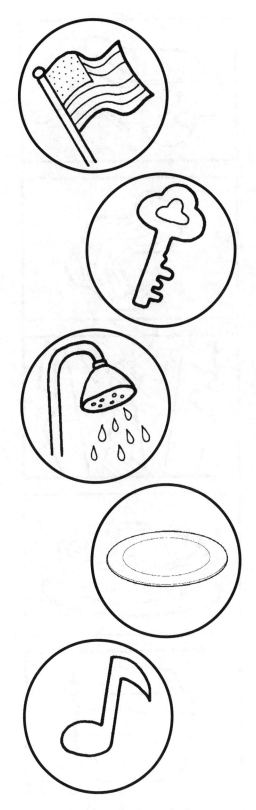

Rhyme the Pictures

1. Draw a line to the rhyming picture.

2. Color the pictures.

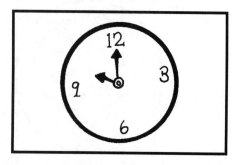

Find My Rhyming Pair.

1. Find the two things that rhyme.

2. Color each pair the same color.

What Am I?

1. Guess what I am.

2. Color the rhyming words. The box below will help you.

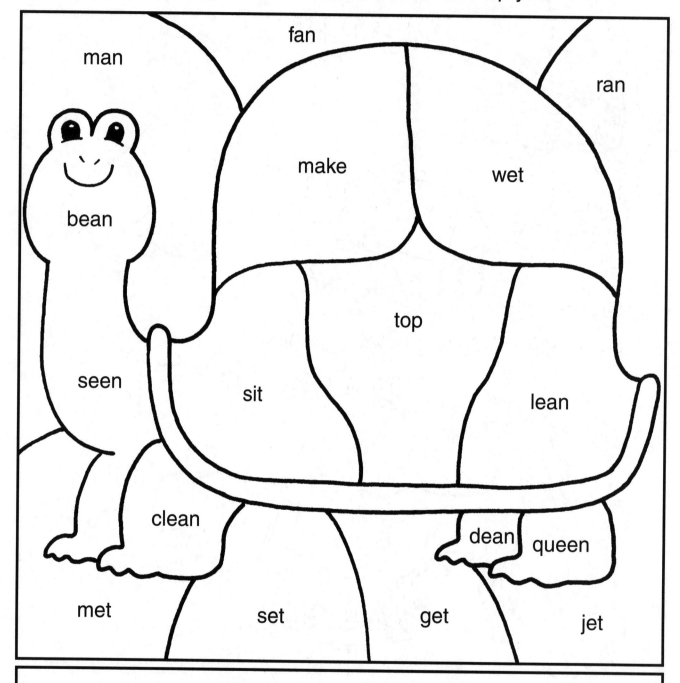

man

fan

ran

bean

make

wet

seen

sit

top

lean

clean

dean

queen

met

set

get

jet

can = blue	hit = purple
let = green	mean = yellow
take = red	mop = orange

My Fat Cat

1. Circle the words that rhyme with cat.
2. Each hidden word begins with a letter from the list.
3. Color the picture around the puzzle.

- **S**
- **M**
- **B**
- **R**
- **H**
- **F**

S	N	F		
L	B	A	D	M
S	A	T	V	A
F	T	R	A	T
H	A	T	J	B

My Pet, Jet

1. Circle the words that rhyme with pet.

2. The beginning letters will help you.

3. Color the picture around the puzzle.

- **M**
- **S**
- **J**
- **L**
- **G**
- **W**

L	E	T	S	Y	U
G	B	W	E	T	V
S	G	E	T	J	K
F	T	R	A	E	T
H	A	M	E	T	F

Making Rhyming Words

Add the first letter to the words below to make words that rhyme with the first word. Look at the pictures for clues.

1. cat

___ at

___ at

2. hog

___ og

___ og

3. man

___ an

___ an

4. pop

___ op

___ op

5. dig

___ ig

___ ig

6. ten

___ en

___ en

Rhyme Time

- Think of a word that rhymes with each picture.
- Write the word.
- Draw the picture.

1.
dish

___ ish

2.
star

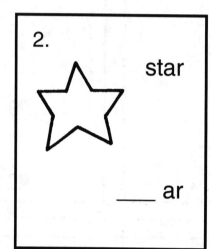

___ ar

3.
man

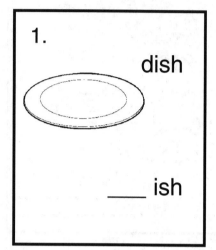

___ an

4.
wig

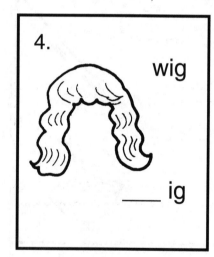

___ ig

5.
og

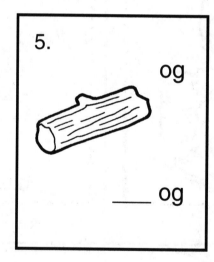

___ og

6.
lake

___ ake

7.
jet

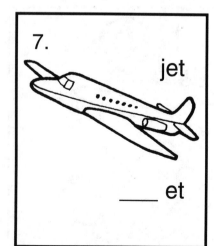

___ et

8.
ten

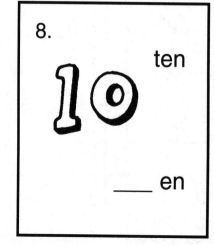

___ en

9.
mat

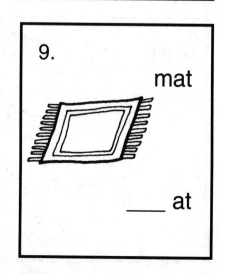

___ at

Above or Below

Decide whether the bird is above or below. Circle your answer.

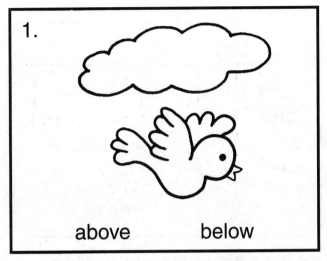

1.

above   below

2.

above   below

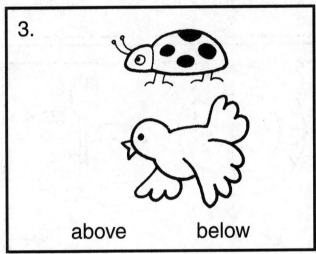

3.

above   below

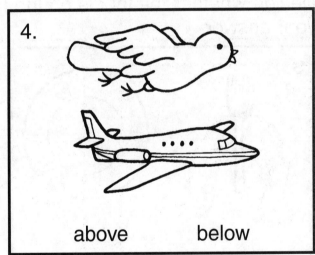

4.

above   below

Draw a star above the box.

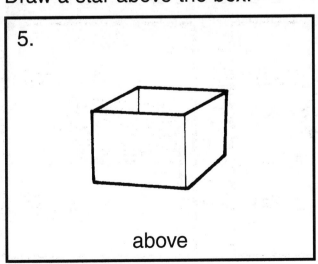

5.

above

Draw a star below the box.

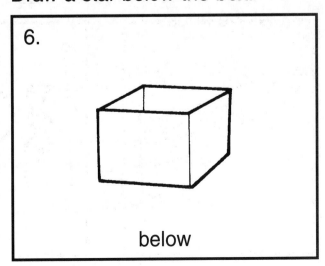

6.

below

Left or Right

Decide whether the bear is on the left or on the right of the box. Circle your answer.

1.

left   right

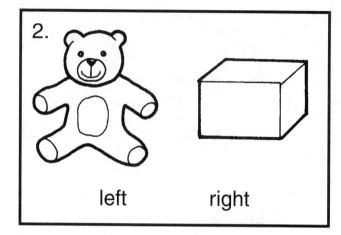

2.

left   right

Decide whether the fork is on the left or the right of the plate. Circle your answer.

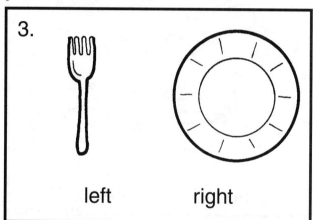

3.

left   right

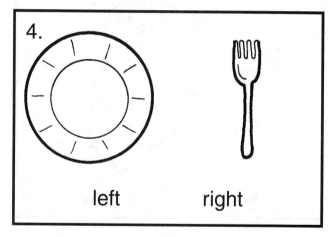

4.

left   right

5. Draw a tree on the left side of the house.

6. Draw a tree on the right side of the house.

In or Out

Decide whether each object is in or out. Circle the correct word.

1.

in   out

1.

in   out

1.

in   out

1.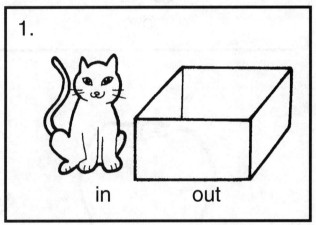

in   out

5. Draw a star in the box.

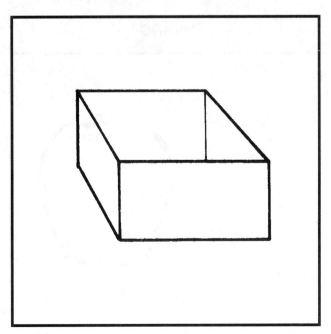

6. Draw a star out of the box.

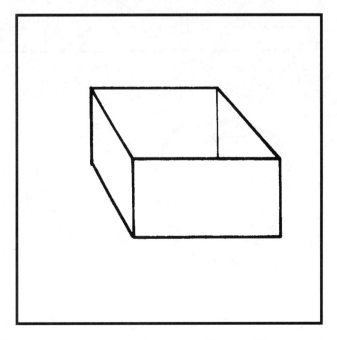

Following Directions

Follow the direction in each box by drawing a worm.

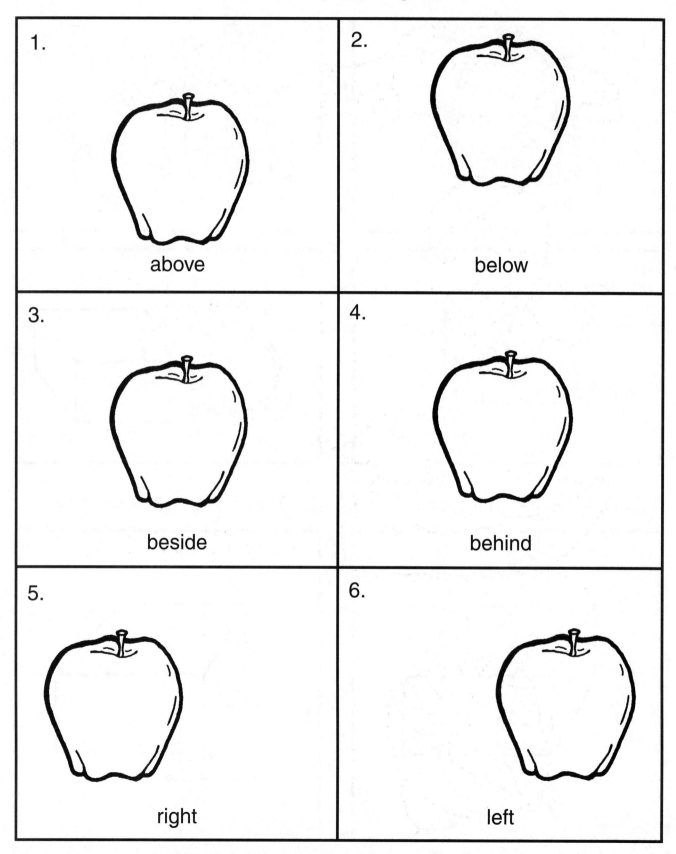

1.

above

2.

below

3.

beside

4.

behind

5.

right

6.

left

Picture-Word Connections

Draw a line to connect each picture to the matching word.

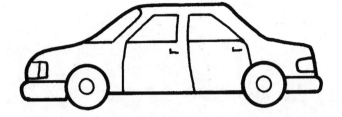

duck

top

man

car

Connecting Pictures to Words

Draw a line to connect each picture to the matching word.

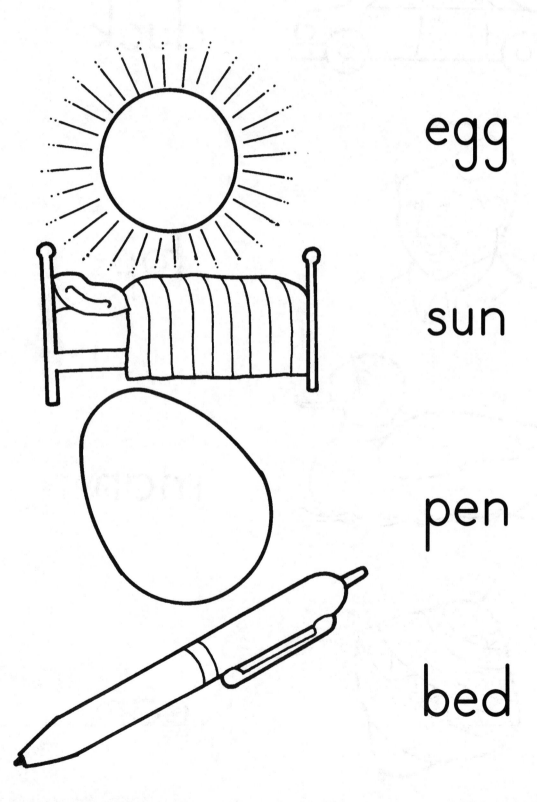

egg

sun

pen

bed

Picture-Word Connections

Draw a line to connect each picture to the matching word.

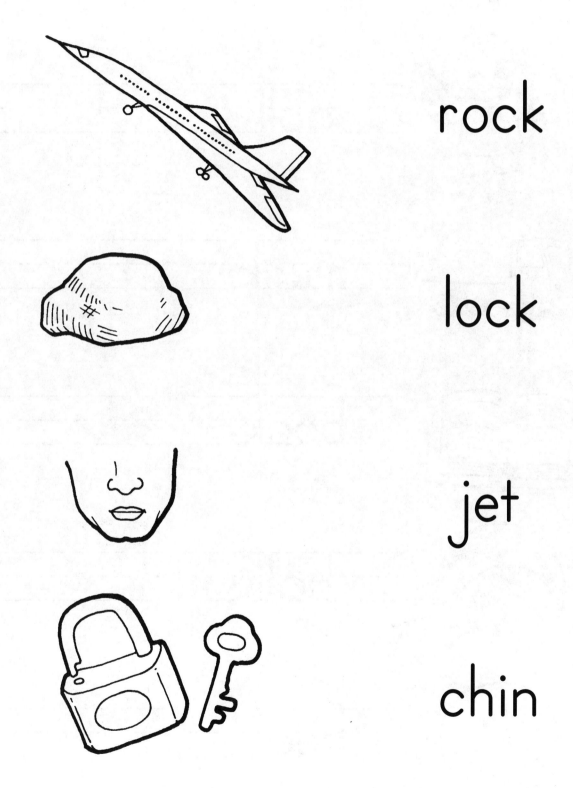

rock

lock

jet

chin

Toy Chest

Use your best printing to write the words.

Color the pictures.

The Zoo

- Use your best printing to write the words.
- Color the pictures.

zebra

giraffe

ape

elephant

monkey

Fruit Basket

- Use your best printing to write the words.
- Color the pictures.

apple

banana

pear

cherries

orange

Animal Names

Print the correct name on each line. Color the pictures.

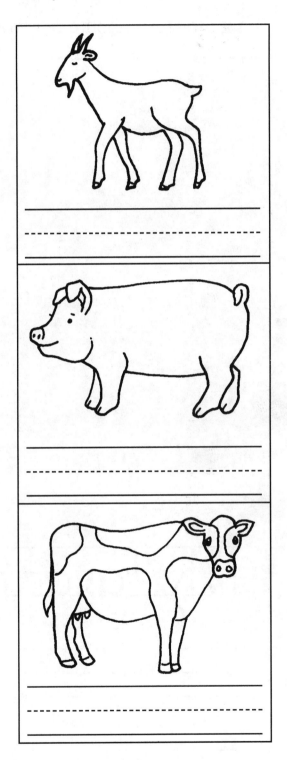

Word Bank

horse   sheep   pig   goat   cow   hen

My Favorite Food

Write some words that finish the sentence below.

Draw a picture about your words.

My favorite food is _____

_____

_____

_____

_____

When I Grow Up

Write some words that finish the sentence below.

Draw a picture about your words.

When I grow up

Playtime

Write some words that finish the sentence below.

Draw a picture about your words.

I like to play with

What I Saw

Write some words that finish the sentence below.

Draw a picture about your words.

Today I saw

My Wish

Write some words that finish the sentence below.

Draw a picture about your words.

I wish I could _____

Cookies

Write a story about the picture.

_____

- -

_____

- -

_____

- -

_____

- -

_____

- -

_____

Dinosaurs

Write a story about the picture.

The Zoo

Write a story about the picture.

_____

- -

_____

- -

_____

- -

_____

- -

_____

- -

Weather

Write a story about the picture.

_____

- -

_____

- -

_____

- -

_____

- -

_____

- -

Pirates

Write a story about the picture.

_____
- -
_____

_____
- -
_____

_____
- -
_____

_____
- -
_____

"Little Miss Muffet"

Little Miss Muffet

Sat on a tuffet,

Eating her curds and whey;

Along came a spider

Who sat down beside her

And frightened Miss Muffet away.

Answer the following questions. Circle the correct answer. Color the picture.

1. Miss Muffet was eating:

2. What sat beside her?

3. Did the spider stand?   YES   NO

4. Miss Muffet was _____ by the spider.

5. Miss Muffet:

Guess the Small Animal

Connect the dots. Color.

- I have eight eyes in my head.
- I have eight legs.
- I spin a silk web.
- I eat insects.

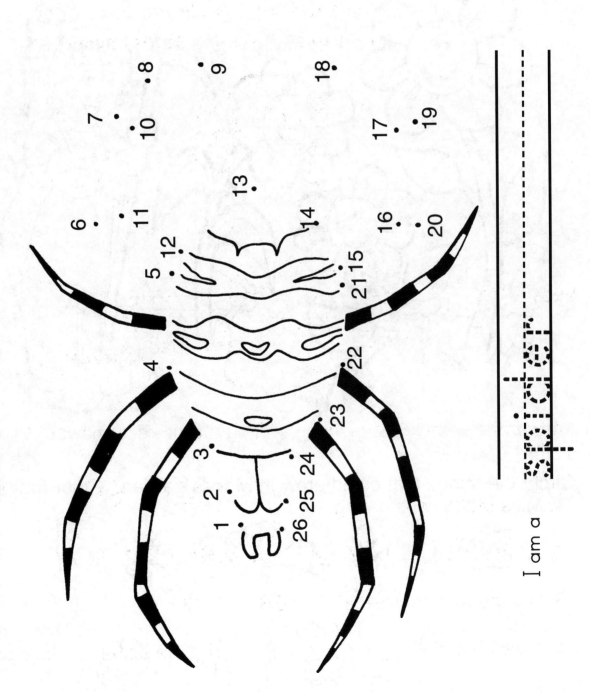

I am a spider

"Mary, Mary, Quite Contrary"

Mary, Mary, quite contrary,

How does your garden grow?

With silver bells and cockle shells

And pretty maids all in a row.

Circle the things that could grow in Mary's garden. Color the picture.

Mary's Garden

Color things in Mary's garden using the color code.

red　　　　　　blue　　　　　　yellow

"Little Bo-Peep"

Little Bo-Peep has lost her sheep,

And doesn't know where to find them;

Leave them alone and they'll come home,

Wagging their tails behind them.

Where Are Little Bo-Peep's Sheep?

Find the sheep.

Circle and color them.

Little Bo-Peep's Sheep

Color by numbers.

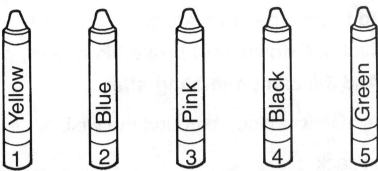

"Jack and Jill"

Jack and Jill ran up a hill,

To fetch a pail of water;

Jack fell down, and broke his crown,

And Jill came tumbling after.

Read the sentence. Draw a blue O around the well.

Draw a green X on Jack.

Draw a red square around the pail.

Fetch a Pail of Water

Help Jack and Jill get up the hill.

"Peter, Peter, Pumpkin Eater"

Peter, Peter, pumpkin eater,

Had a wife and couldn't keep her;

He put her in a pumpkin shell,

And there he kept her very well.

Write the numbers 1, 2, and 3 in the circles to show the order of the poem.

Had a wife and couldn't keep her; Peter, Peter, pumpkin eater, **He put her in a pumpkin shell and there he kept her very well.**

Peter's Pumpkin Shell

1. Read the words.

2. Color.

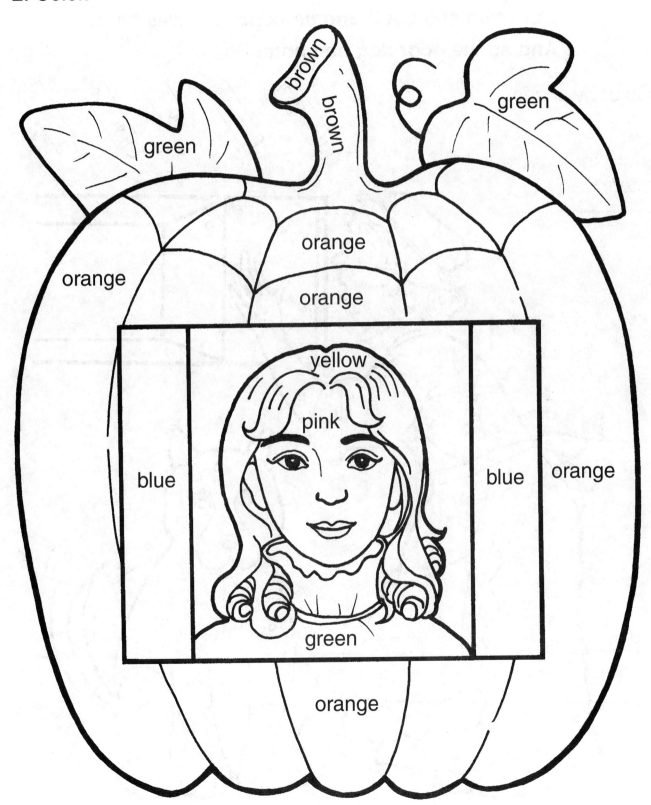

" Old Mother Hubbard"

Old Mother Hubbard went to the cupboard,

To fetch her poor dog a bone;

But when she got there the cupboard was bare,

And so the poor dog had none.

Color by shape.

Old Mother Hubbard's Dog

Color and cut out the dog picture pieces.

Glue the pieces in order, into a stand-up dog figure.

"Little Jack Horner"

Little Jack Horner sat in the corner,

Eating a Christmas pie;

He put in his thumb, and pulled out a plum,

And said, "What a good boy am I!"

Connect the dots.

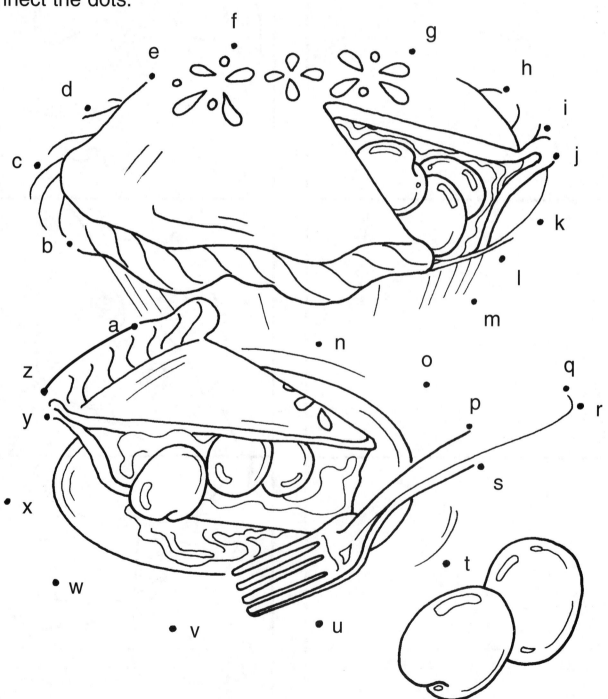

He Stuck in His Thumb...

Find the plum message. Color the picture.

1	6	2		8	10	4	4	3	2

7	10	9		1		8	4	10	5 ___!

"Humpty Dumpty"

Humpty Dumpty sat on a wall,

Humpty Dumpty had a great fall.

All the king's horses and all the king's men,

Couldn't put Humpty together again.

Color the Humpty Dumpty.

Color by shape.

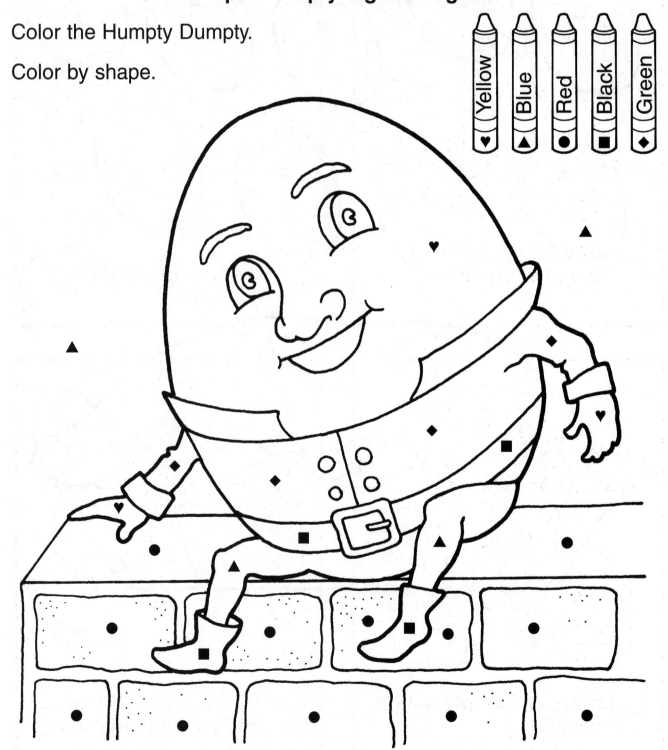

Humpty Dumpty's Fall

Write the numbers 1, 2, 3, and 4 to show the order of the poem.

☐ **Couldn't put Humpty together again.**

☐ **Humpty Dumpty had a great fall.**

☐ **Humpty Dumpty sat on a wall,**

☐ **All the king's horses and all the king's men,**

"Little Boy Blue"

Little Boy Blue, come blow your horn,
The sheep's in the meadow, the cow's in the corn;
But where is the boy who looks after the sheep?
He's under the haystack fast asleep.

1. Read and color.

2. Then color the rest of the picture.

Color the   yellow.   Color the   black.

Color the   brown.   Color the   orange.

"Little Boy Blue"

Circle the things that happen in the rhyme. Color.

"One, Two, Buckle My Shoe"

Trace the numbers.

1, 2,

Buckle my shoe.

3, 4,

Shut the door.

5, 6,

Pick up sticks.

7, 8,

Lay them straight.

9, 10,

A big fat hen.

"Hey Diddle, Diddle"

Read the poem. Color the pictures.

Hey Diddle, Diddle
The cat and the fiddle,

The cow jumped over the moon.

The little dog laughed to
see such sport,

And the dish ran away
with the spoon.

"Jack Be Nimble"

Jack be nimble,

Jack be quick,

Jack jump over the candlestick.

Color Jack and the pictures that begin with "J".

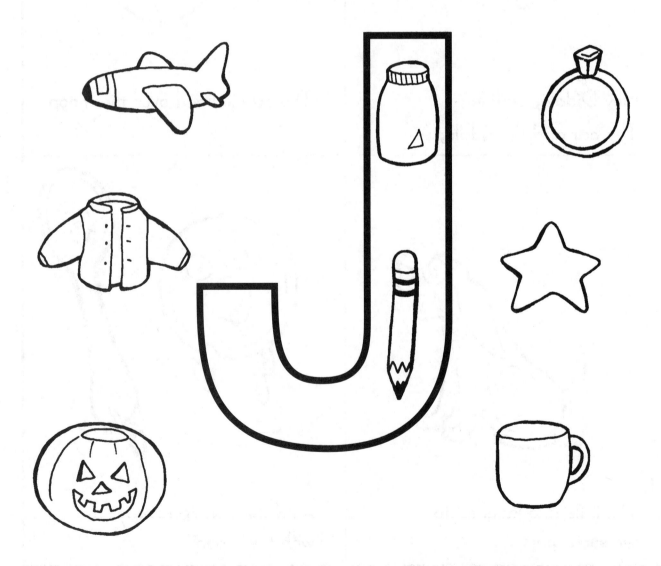

"Pease Porridge"

Pease porridge hot,

Pease porridge cold,

Pease porridge in the pot, nine days old.

Some like it hot,

Some like it cold,

Some like it in the pot, nine days old.

◆　◆　◆

Color cold pictures blue. Color hot pictures red.

ice cube

soup

ice-cream cone

sun

candle

snowman

"Baa, Baa, Black Sheep"

Baa, Baa, black sheep,

Have you any wool?

Yes, sir, yes, sir,

Three bags full;

One for my master,

One for my dame,

And one for the little boy

Who lives down the lane.

• Count.   • Print numbers.   • Color.

"The Mouse Ran Up the Clock"

Hickory, Dickory, Dock!
The mouse ran up the clock;
The clock struck one,
The mouse ran down,
Hickory, Dickory, Dock!

Connect the dots.

"The Three Little Kittens"

The three little kittens,

They lost their mittens,

And they began to cry.

"Oh, mother dear, we sadly fear,

Our mittens we have lost."

"What! Lost your mittens, you naughty kittens!

Then you shall have no pie."

- Match the mittens.
- Color each pair alike.

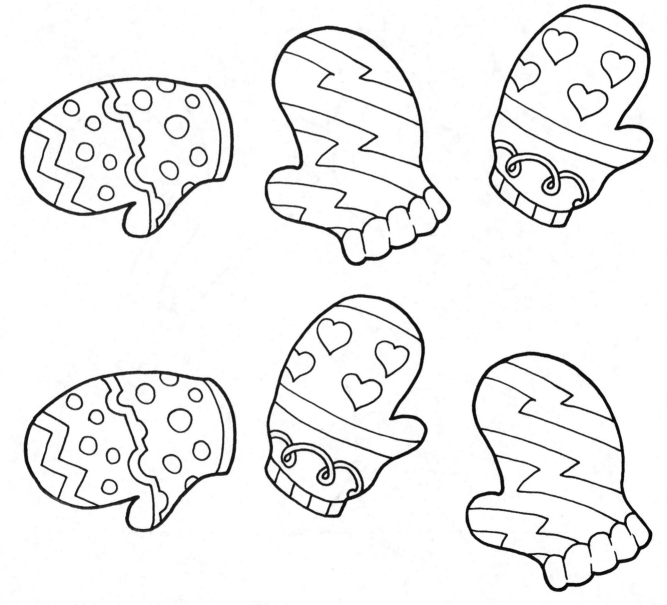

"Rain, Rain"

Rain, rain, go away,

Come again another day,

Little Johnny wants to play.

Color all the things you can do in the rain.

Fairy Tales

Kindergarten students should be familiar with a variety of folk and fairy tales. This section of the book presents activities for several fairy tales. Additional activities and sources are listed below.

"The Little Red Hen"

The Little Red Hen retold by Lucinda McQueen (Scholastic, Inc., 1993).

The Little Red Hen by Paul Galdone (Houghton Mifflin, 1985).

The Little Red Hen by Margot Zemach (Farrar, Strauss & Giroux, 1983).

What to Talk About

- Have your child think of times when he or she has helped. Discuss the benefits of helping.
- Ask whether your child thinks the duck, cat, and dog should be able to eat some bread.

Activities

- Have your child help you make a loaf of bread.
- Read the chant on page 136. Your child can help read the repetitive portions of the text.
- After your child has colored and cut out the pictures on page 137, help him or her arrange the pictures in the correct sequence.

"The Three Little Pigs"

The Three Little Pigs by Paul Galdone (Houghton Miffin, 1984).

The Three Little Pigs by Margot Zemach (Sunburst, 1991).

The Three Little Pigs by James Marshall (Puffin, 1996).

What to Talk About

- Discuss the different types of materials the pigs used to build their houses. Of what kind of material is your house made?
- Ask how your child felt when the wolf fell in the boiling water. Be sure to distinguish between fantasy and reality.

Activities

- Read a variation of the story like *The True Story of the Three Little Pigs written by A. Wolf*, as told to Jon Scieszka (Viking Children's Books, 1992) or *The Three Little Wolves and the Big Bad Pig* by Eugene Triviza (Heinemann Young Books, 1993). Compare and contrast the various stories.
- Read the chant on page 138. Ask your child to read the repetitive parts of the text.
- Help your child complete the story map on page 139.

"The Gingerbread Man"

The Gingerbread Man by Eric A. Kimmel (Holiday House, 1994).

The Gingerbread Man by Richard Scarry (Golden Book Publishing Co. Inc., 1997).

The Gingerbread Man by Karen Schmidt (Scholastic, 1986).

The Gingerbread Boy by David Cutts (Troll Associates, 1989).

What to Talk About

- Your child may be upset that the Gingerbread Man gets eaten. If so, talk about why that might be upsetting.

Fairy Tales (cont.)

What to Talk About *(cont.)*

- Ask how your child felt when the Gingerbread Man jumped up, talked, and ran away. Could this really happen?
- Talk about the fox. How did he manage to outsmart everyone else who wanted to eat the Gingerbread Man?
- What lesson does the story teach about being boastful?

Activities

- Read the chant on page 140. Ask your child to read the repetitive part.
- Play the board game on page 141 with your child. You will need a die and some things to use as a space markers.

"The Hare and the Tortoise"

The Tortoise and the Hare by Betty Miles *(Aladdin Paperbacks, 1998).*

The Tortoise and the Hare adapted by Janet Stevens (Holiday House, 1985).

The Tortoise and the Hare by Carla Dijs (Little Simon, 1997).

What to Talk About

- Who were the main characters in the story? Where did the story take place? Who won the race? How was the tortoise able to win?
- Look at the illustrations carefully to identify the many types of animals in the book. Discuss whether they look real or make-believe. Ask your child to tell you how he or she knows.

Activities

- Read the Hare Versus the Tortoise Cheer on page 142. Ask your child to read the repetitive lines.
- Have your child do research on an animal. Help him or her fill out the Animal Research Report on page 143.

"The Three Billy Goats Gruff"

The Three Billy Goats Gruff by Janet Stevens (Harcourt Brace Jovanovich, 1990).

The Three Billy Goats Gruff by Glen Rounds (Holiday House, 1994).

The Three Billy-Goats Gruff by Ellen Appleby (Scholastic, 1993).

What to Talk About

- What was the problem in this story? How was the problem solved?
- Talk about trolls and name some other imaginary creatures found in folktales and fairy tales (fairies, witches, elves, etc.).
- Talk about how goats will eat almost anything. Ask what the goats in this story wanted to eat.

Activities

- Build a bridge with your child. You can use any materials available such as blocks, milk cartons, or Legos.
- Read the chant on page 144. Ask your child to participate by reading the repetitive part.
- Have your child color and cut out the character pieces on page 145. Attach a wooden stick to the back of each character. Help your child retell the story, using the characters.

The Little Red Hen

Little Red Hen has found some wheat.

"Who will help me plant the wheat, so we may have bread to eat?"
"Not I!" said the duck. "Not I!" said the cat. "Not I!" said the dog.
"Then I shall do it myself," said the Little Red Hen.

"Who will help me water the wheat, so we may have bread to eat?"
"Not I!" said the duck. "Not I!" said the cat. "Not I!" said the dog.
"Then I shall do it myself," said the Little Red Hen.

"Who will help me hoe the wheat, so we may have bread to eat?"
"Not I!" said the duck. "Not I!" said the cat. "Not I!" said the dog.
"Then I shall do it myself," said the Little Red Hen.

"Who will help me cut the wheat, so we may have bread to eat?"
"Not I!" said the duck. "Not I!" said the cat. "Not I!" said the dog.
"Then I shall do it myself," said the Little Red Hen.

"Who will help me grind the wheat, so we may have bread to eat?'
"Not I!" said the duck. "Not I!" said the cat. "Not I!" said the dog.
"Then I shall do it myself," said the Little Red Hen.

"Who will help me make the bread?"
"Not I!" said the duck. "Not I!" said the cat. "Not I!" said the dog.
"Then I shall do it myself," said the Little Red Hen.

When the bread was done, her friends all wanted to eat.
But the Little Red Hen ate the whole treat!

The Little Red Hen Story Sequencing

Directions: Color and cut the pictures along the dotted lines. Then arrange the pictures in the correct sequence.

The Little Red Hen watered the wheat.

The Little Red Hen ate the bread.

The Little Red Hen made the bread.

The Little Red Hen found some wheat.

The Little Red Hen planted the wheat.

The Little Red Hen cut the wheat.

The Three Little Pigs

One pig built his house of straw.
Oh, no! Oh, no!

One pig built his house of sticks.
Oh, no! Oh, no!

One pig built his house of bricks.
Smart pig! Smart pig!

Then the wolf came to blow them down.
Huff, puff! Huff, puff!

Down went the houses of straw and sticks.
Huff, puff! Huff, puff!

But he couldn't blow down that house of bricks.
Huff, puff! Huff, puff!

Who's afraid of the big bad wolf?
Not us! Not us!

The Three Little Pigs Story Map

Directions: Color the pictures below. Cut along the dotted lines. Glue the pictures in the correct boxes on the map to retell the story.

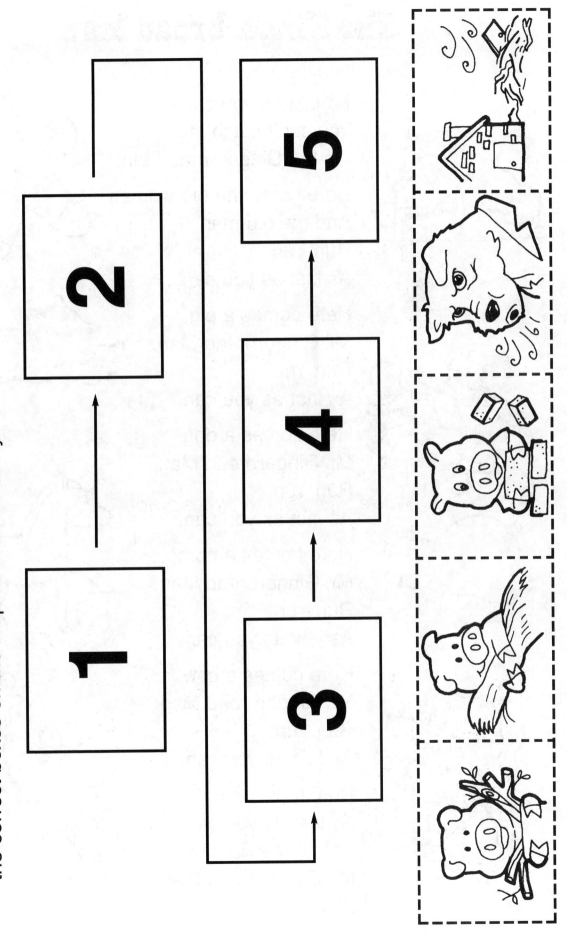

The Gingerbread Man

Run, run,
As fast as you can.
You can't catch me,
I'm the Gingerbread Man!

Here come the old woman
And the old man.
Run, run,
As fast as you can.

Here comes a pig,
Mr. Gingerbread Man.
Run, run,
As fast as you can.

Here comes a dog,
Mr. Gingerbread Man.
Run, run,
As fast as you can.

Here comes a horse,
Mr. Gingerbread Man.
Run, run,
As fast as you can.

Here comes a cow,
Mr. Gingerbread Man.
Run, run,
As fast as you can.

Run, run,
As fast as you can.
But the fox caught you,
Mr. Gingerbread Man!

The Gingerbread Man Game Board

Materials: a die and space markers

Directions:

Roll a die to find out how many spaces to move. The winner is the person who reaches the gingerbread house first.

Start

Run, run, as fast as you can! Take another turn.

You are getting tired. Go back one space.

Look out for the Fox! Lose a turn.

You are almost there. Take another turn.

Finish

The Hare and the Tortoise Cheer

Hare and Tortoise had a race.
Go! Go!
Slow and steady wins the race.

Hare was fast. Tortoise was slow.
Go! Go!
Slow and steady wins the race.

Hare was running. Tortoise was walking.
Go! Go!
Slow and steady wins the race.

Hare was winning. Tortoise kept walking.
Go! Go!
Slow and steady wins the race.

Hare was sleeping. Tortoise kept walking.
Go! Go!
Slow and steady wins the race.

Hare woke up. Tortoise kept walking.
Go! Go!
Slow and steady wins the race.

Tortoise kept walking and won the race.
Hooray! Hooray!
Slow and steady won the race!

Animal Research Report

Researched by _____

This is a real animal.

It is a _____.

[empty box]

It lives _____.

It has _____ legs.

It eats _____.

Its babies are called _____.

I also found out that it _____.

The Three Billy Goats Gruff

The three goats are hungry
For something to eat.
Trip, trap,
Trip, trap.

But under the bridge
Watch out for the troll!
Trip, trap,
Trip, trap.

Over the bridge
The little goat crosses.
Trip, trap,
Trip, trap.

Over the bridge
The second goat crosses.
Trip, trap,
Trip, trap.

Over the bridge
The biggest goat crosses.
Trip, trap,
Trip, trap.

Off the bridge goes the troll
And the goats have their lunch.
Trip, trap,
Trip, trap.

The three goats' story
Has come to an end.
Snip, snap, snout.
This tale's told out.

Character Patterns

Directions: Color and cut out these characters. Staple them to wooden sticks. Use for retelling the story.

Colors

Color each balloon a different color. Name the color you used for each balloon.

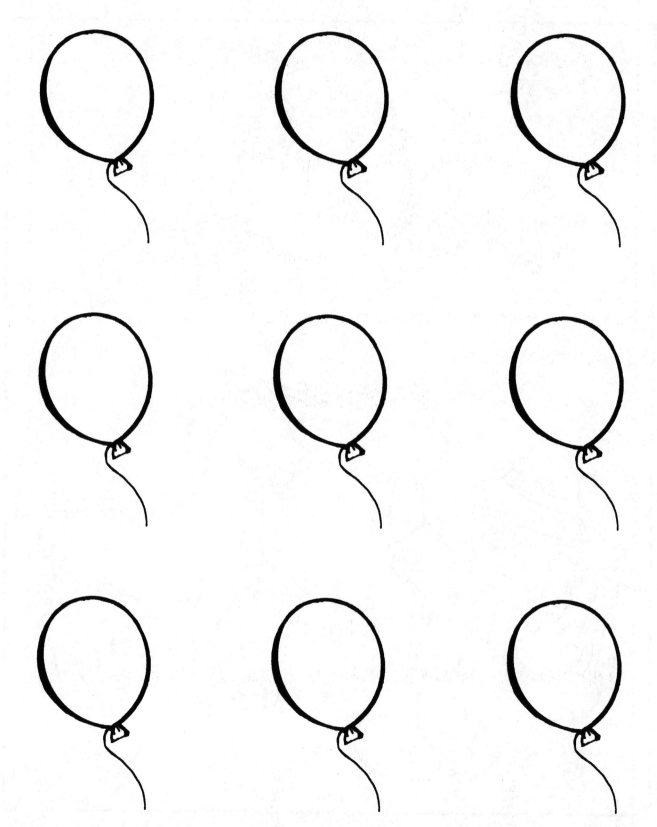

Rainbow Colors

Trace the names and color the rainbow.

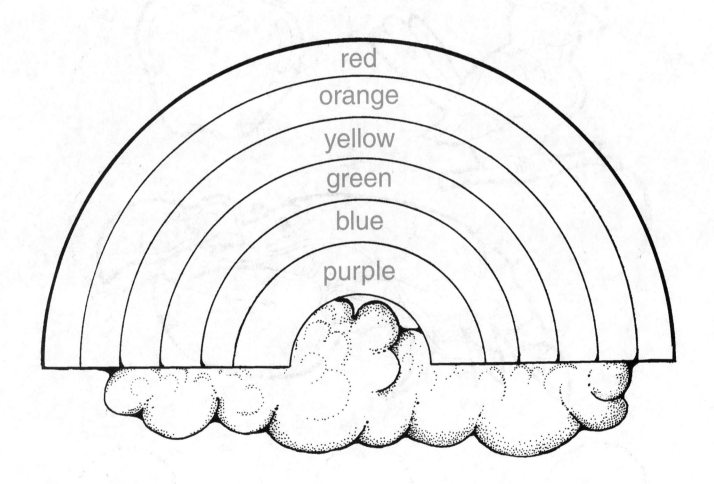

The Color Red

Trace the words below. Color the pictures red.

R̶e̶d̶

r̶e̶d̶

The Color Orange

Trace the words below. Color the pictures orange.

Orange

orange

The Color Yellow

Trace the words below. Color the pictures yellow.

Yellow

yellow

The Color Green

Trace the words below. Color the pictures green.

Green

green

The Color Blue

Trace the words below. Color the pictures blue.

The Color Purple

Trace the words below. Color the pictures purple.

Purple

purple

The Color Brown

Trace the words below. Color the pictures brown.

Brown

brown

The Color Black

Trace the words below. Color the pictures black.

Black

black

Color Match

 Draw lines to match the color words to the pictures.

 Color the pictures.

red

blue

yellow

orange

green

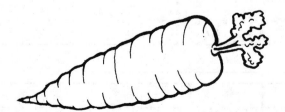

More Color Match

 Draw lines to match the color words to the pictures.

 Color the pictures.

purple

brown

pink

black

white

Color a Boat

Trace the boat. Draw a flag. Color.

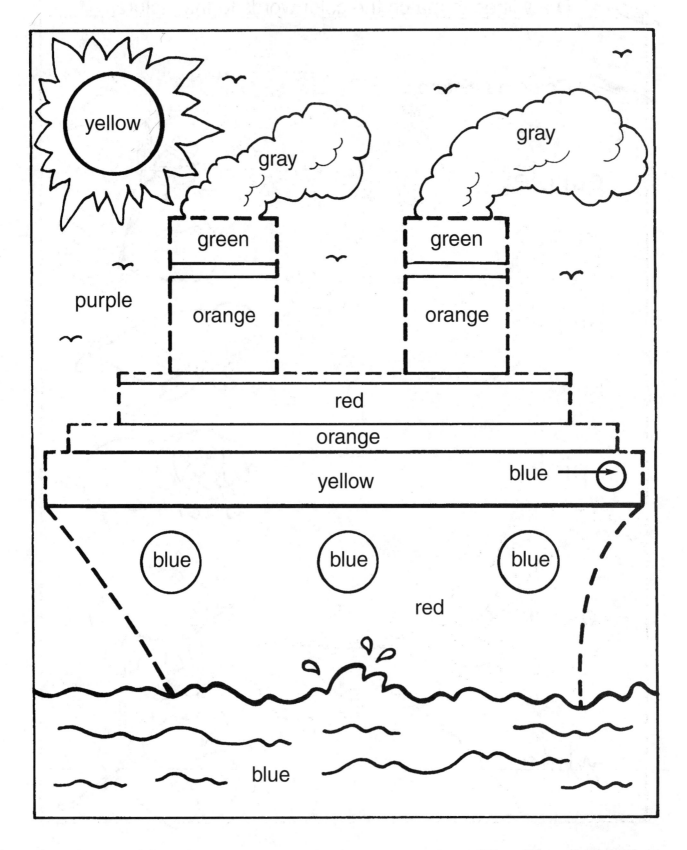

Somersaults

Color the picture.

The Fruit Tree

Color the fruit using the color code.

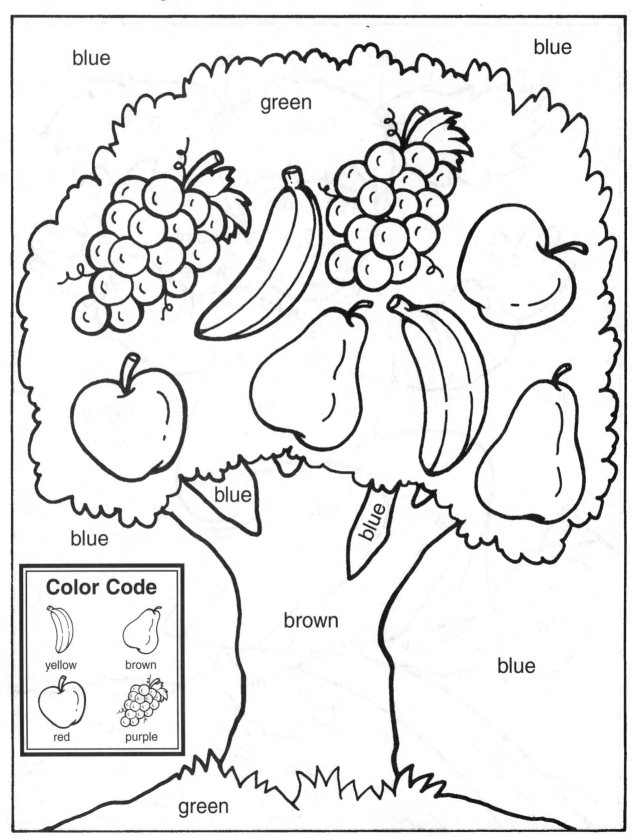

Cat and Mouse

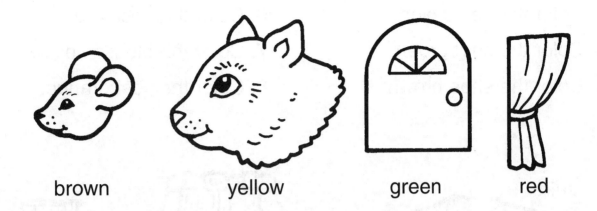

brown   yellow   green   red

1. Color the objects above.

2. Color the objects in the picture below the same as above.

Hang Up Your Clothes

1. Color the dress pink.

2. Color the pants blue.

3. Color the shirt green.

4. Color the shoe brown.

5. Color the hat purple.

6. Color the sock red.

7. Color the blouse yellow.

8. Color the vest orange.

shirt

pants

sock

shoe

vest

dress

blouse

hat

Let's Make a Hamburger

1. Color the top bun and bottom bun light brown.

2. Color the meat dark brown.

3. Color the onion purple.

4. Color the pickles green.

5. Color the tomato red.

6. Color the lettuce green.

7. Color the french fries yellow.

8. Color the catsup, inside the bottle, red.

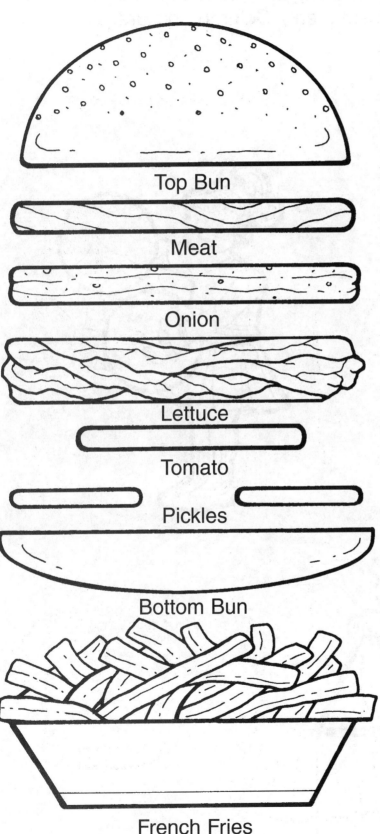

Top Bun

Meat

Onion

Lettuce

Tomato

Pickles

Bottom Bun

French Fries

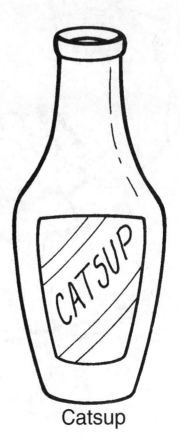

Catsup

Strike Up the Band

Trace each outlined shape with a finger, then trace it with a crayon. Name each shape and the instrument. Color the picture.

Shape Tracing

First, use your finger to trace the shapes. Then use a crayon.

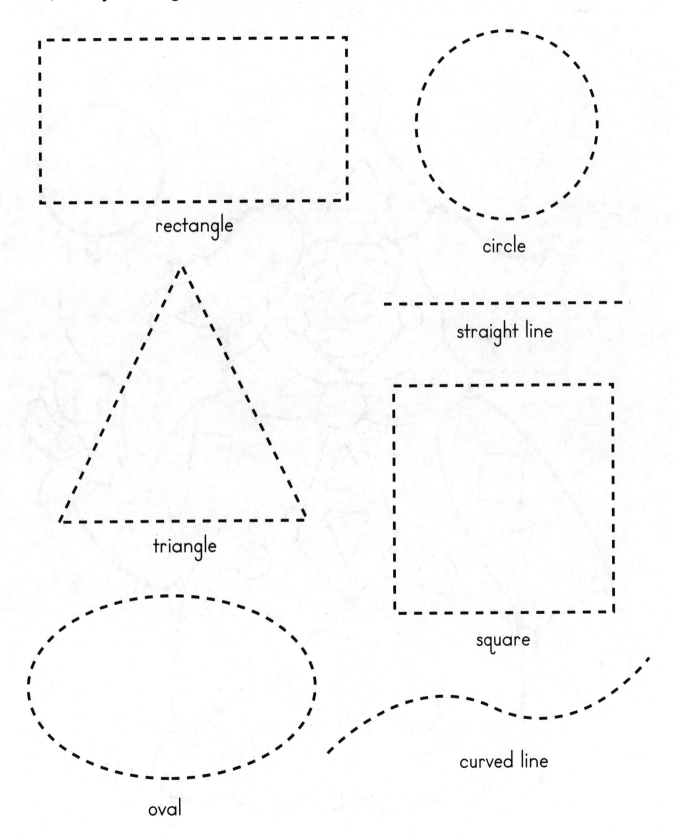

Shape Master—Clown

Find the hidden shapes in the picture of the clown.

Color all the circles red. Color all the squares green. Color all the triangles yellow.

Shapes and Colors

Color the ☐ 's yellow.

Color the ⬭ 's purple.

Color the ◇ 's orange

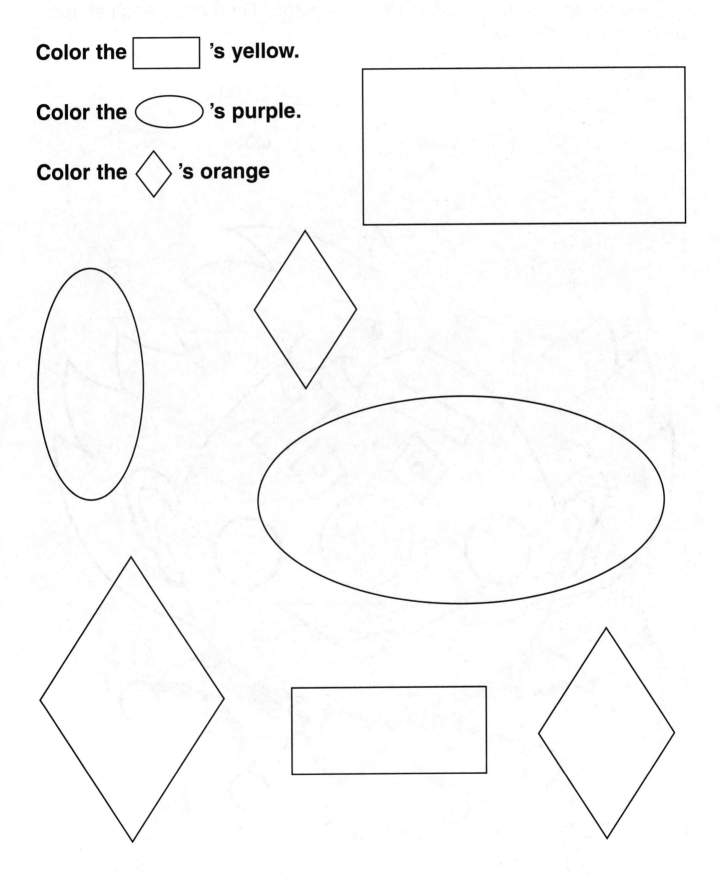

Shapes Clown

Color each shape at the top the correct color. Then color each shape on the picture to match.

Color all the: red   green

   yellow   blue

Find the Shape

Color the matching shape. Name each shape.

Color by Shapes

 Follow the shapes to color the picture.

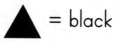 = green   ▲ = black   ● = blue   ♥ = yellow

More Color by Shapes

 Follow the shapes to color the picture.

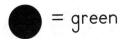 = green 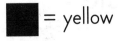 = yellow 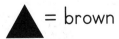 = brown 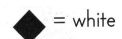 = white

Practice and Learn—Kindergarten

Shape Names

 Draw a line to match each shape to its name. Color the shapes green.

rectangle

heart

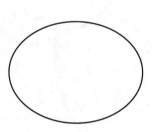

diamond

oval

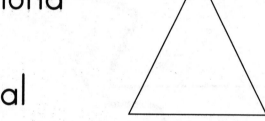

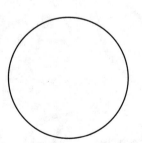

star

square

triangle

circle

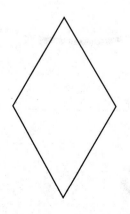

Naming Shapes

 Trace the name under each shape.

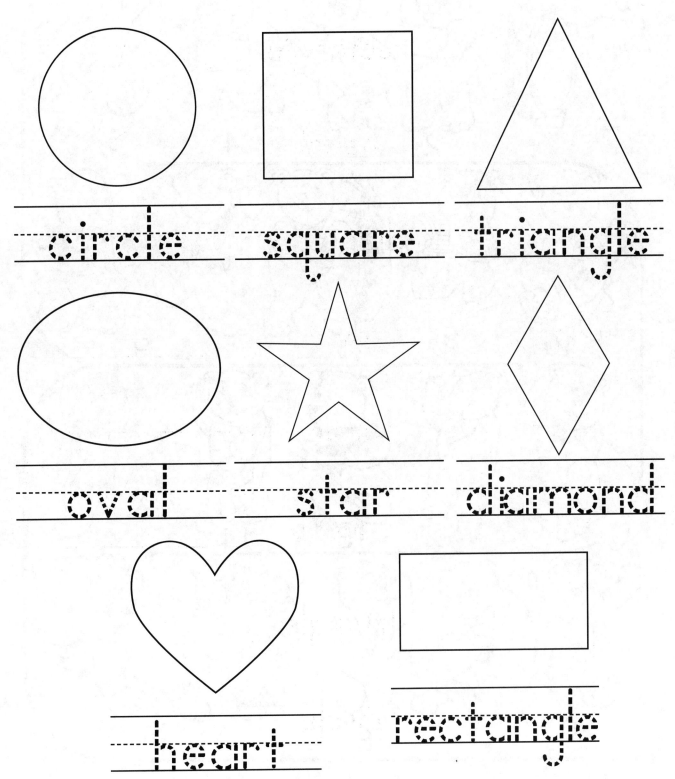

circle square triangle

oval star diamond

heart rectangle

Bears on Parade

The bears are on parade today. Some of them have lost their numbers.
Help them get in order by writing the correct number under each one.

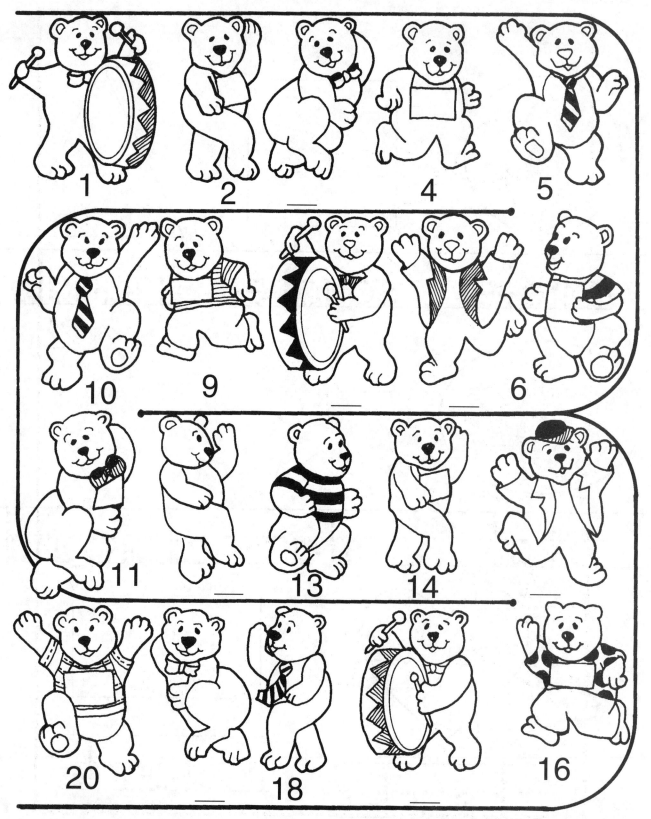

Slow and Easy Wins

To find out who won the race, connect the dots from 1-12. Color the picture.

Dot-to-Dot Number Bear

Follow the dots fo finish the picture.

Another Dot-to-Dot Number Bear

Follow the numbers to finish the picture.

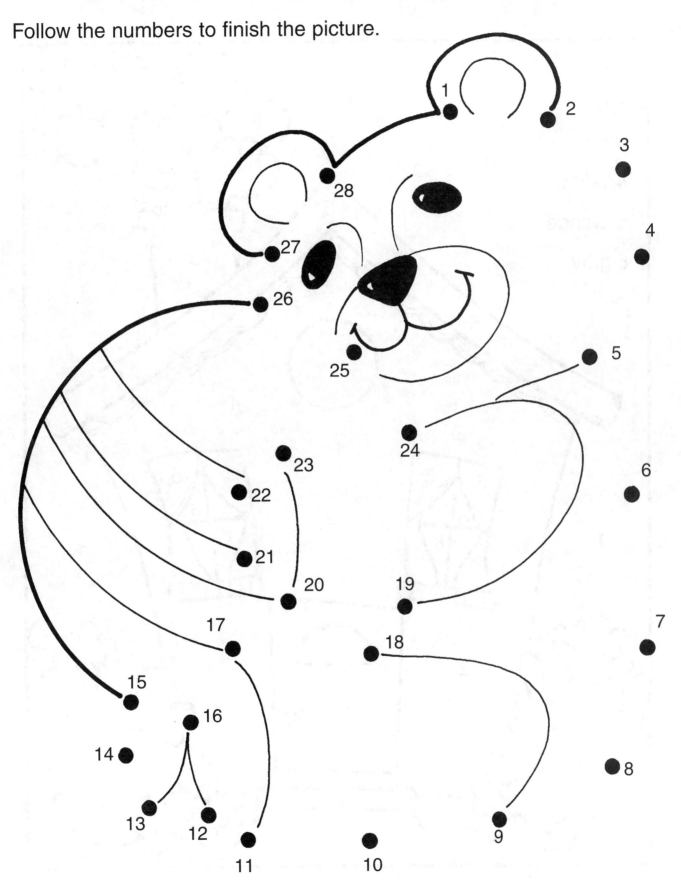

Color by Number

1 blue
2 green
3 red
4 yellow
5 orange
6 gray

Priscilla Peacock

Color key:

1 = red

2 = blue

3 = yellow

4 = green

5 = purple

6 = orange

7 = brown

8 = black

By the Number

Color this picture by using the numbers and colors in the chart.

Color by Number

number	color to use
1	green
2	blue

number	color to use
3	gray
4	brown

Painting the Clubhouse

Color by numbers.

Color key
1 = red
2 = green
3 = blue
4 = yellow
5 = black
6 = brown

Balloon Match

Draw a line from each balloon to its matching number.

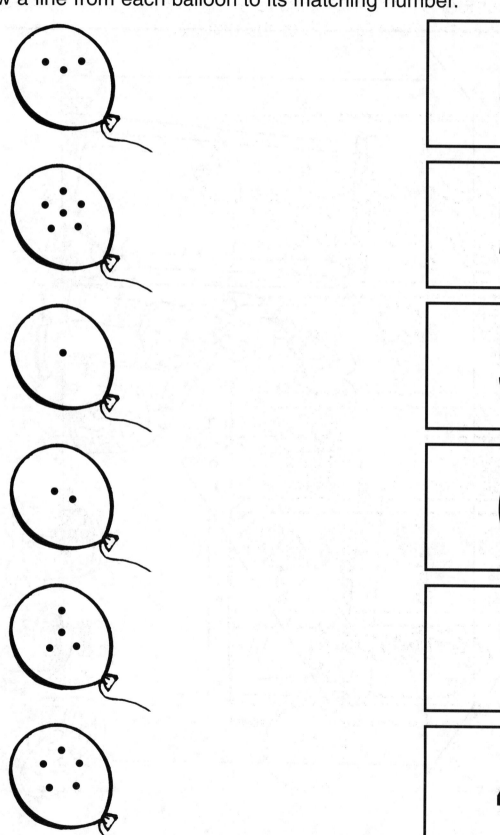

Counting 1-5

Count the number of things on each shelf of the food cart. Draw a line to the numeral that matches. Color the picture.

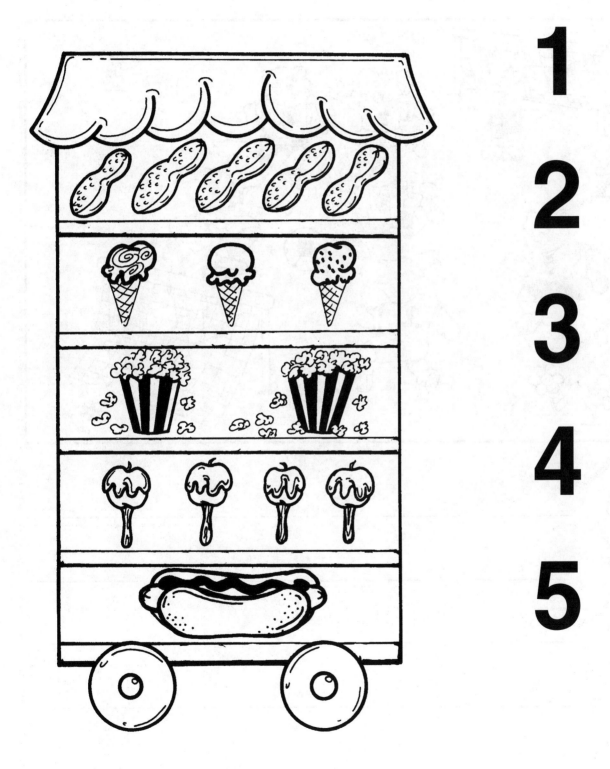

183

Team Numbers

The cats play ball with the dogs.

Draw "X's" to show how many.

 _____

 _____

 _____

_____

_____

0–Zero

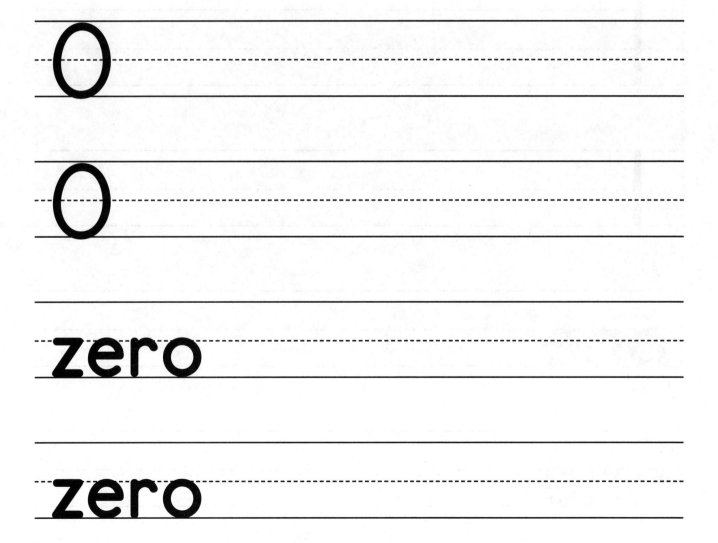

1–One

l

l

one

one

2—Two

2

2

two

two

3–Three

3 -

3 -

three -

three -

4–Four

4

4

four

four

5–Five

5

5

five

five

6—Six

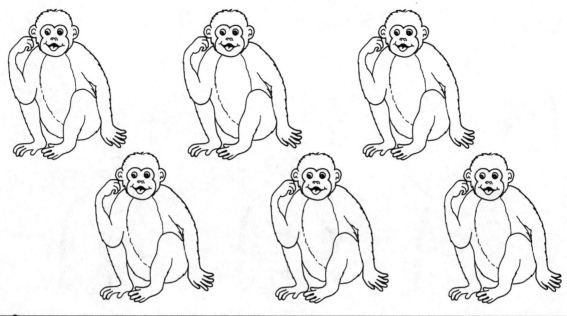

6

6

six

six

7–Seven

7

7

seven

seven

8—Eight

8

8

eight

eight

9–Nine

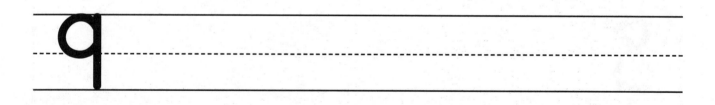

q

q

nine

nine

10–Ten

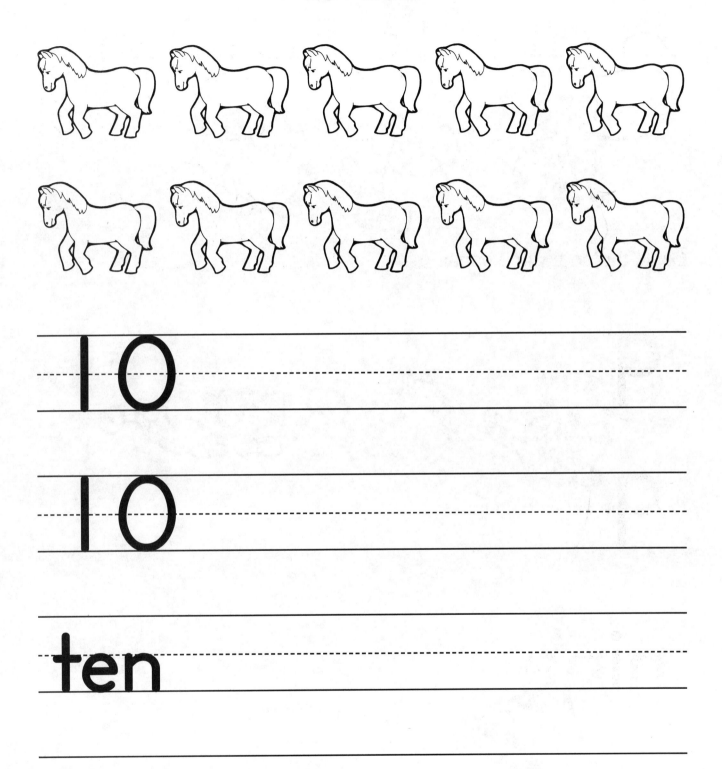

10

10

ten

ten

Zero in on Zero

Circle the dog with 0 spots.

Circle the cat with 0 stripes.

How many stripes
on the dog? _____

How many spots
on the cat? _____

How Many Berries?

Count the berries in the pail.

Write the number under the pail.

Color.

a.

_____

b.

_____

c.

_____

d.

_____

e.

_____

f.

_____

How Many?

Count how many items are in each box. Write the number on the line.

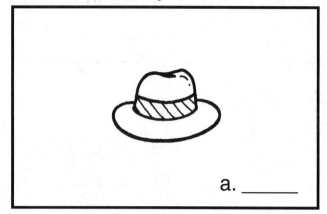

a. _____

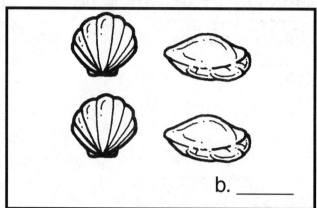

b. _____

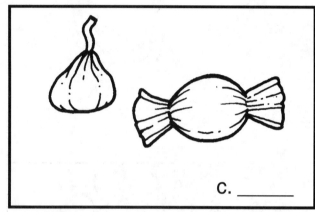

c. _____

d. _____

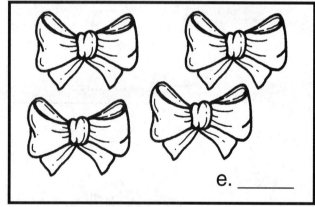

e. _____

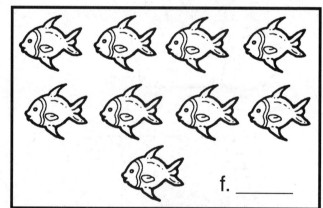

f. _____

g. _____

h. _____

Count the Library Books

Directions: Count the library books in each row. Then write the number in the box.

Count the Objects

Directions: Count the objects. Write the correct number in each box.

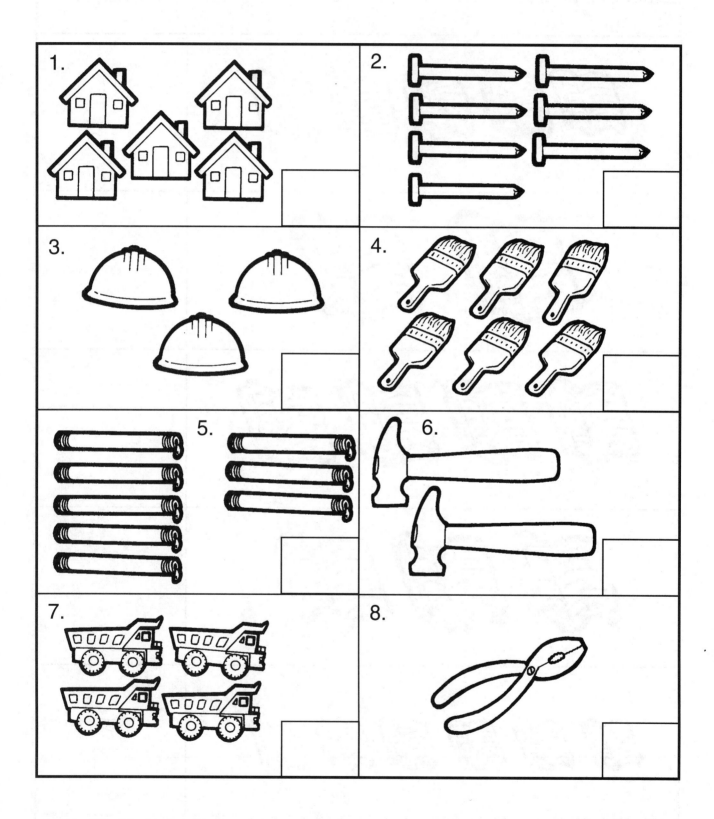

How Many Are There?

Directions: Write the correct numeral in each box.

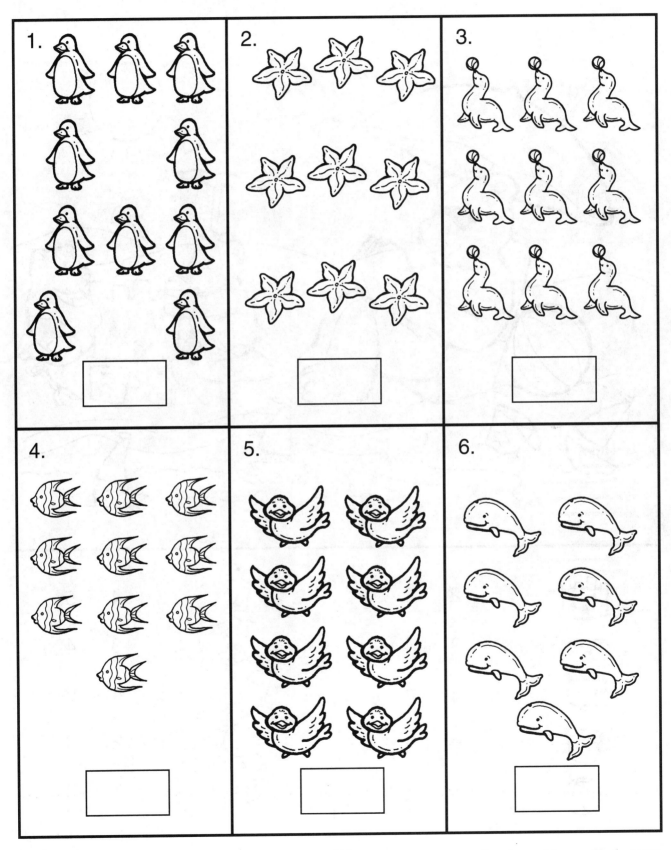

Beach Bears

Circle the numeral that tells how many.

---

  1 2 3

  2 3 4

  3 4 5

  1 2 3

  1 2 3

 3 4 5

 2 3 4

 3 4 5

 1 2 3

  0 1 2

Coloring Fun

Color 3 stars yellow.

Color 2 balls red.

Color 1 bell blue.

Color 3 tops yellow.

Color 4 apples red.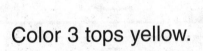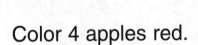

Color 5 hats blue.

1. How many things are yellow? _____ stars + _____ tops = _____

2. How many things are red? _____ apples + _____ balls = _____

3. How many things are blue? _____ bell + _____ hats = _____

Practice and Learn—Kindergarten

Number Names

Match the names to the numbers.

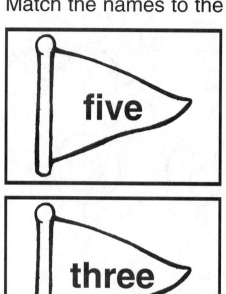

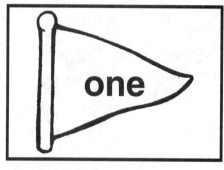

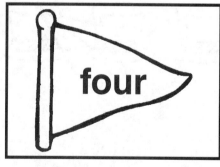

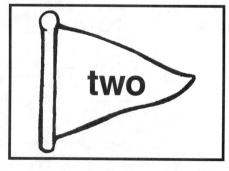

How Many Bees?

1. Count the bees.

2. Write the number in the box at the bottom of the page.

3. Color.

How many bees?

Snowflakes

1. Count the snowflakes.

2. Write the number in the box at the bottom of the page.

3. Color.

How many snowflakes?

Counting People

1. Count the people on or near the bus.
2. Write the number in the box.

Gingerbread House

Write the numerals from 1 to 100.

1	2	3				7	8	9	
11			14	15	16	17		19	20
21				25		27	28	29	30
31		33	34		36			39	
41		43			46	47		49	50
	52	53		55		57		59	
61	62		64		66		68		70
71		73	74		76	77		79	80
81		83			86		88	89	90
91		93	94			96	98		100

Draw It

1. Draw the pictures.

2. Color.

Snowmen

Draw buttons on the snowmen. Use the number to tell you how many buttons to draw.

Apple Trees

Draw apples on the trees. Use the number on the tree to tell you how many apples to draw.

Flying High

Draw bows on the kite strings. Use the number in the box to tell you how many bows to draw.

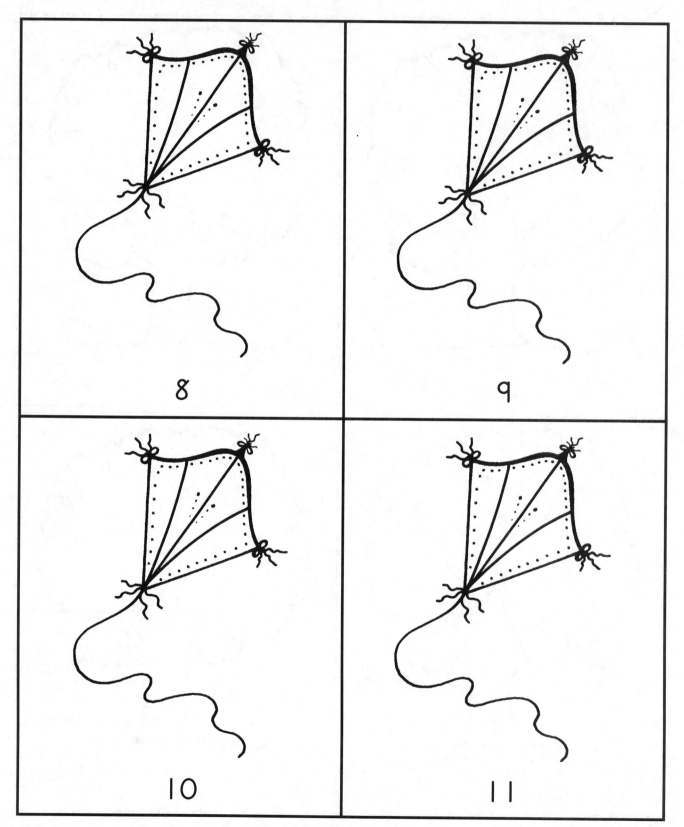

8   q

10   11

Which Has Fewer?

Circle the group that has fewer things in it.

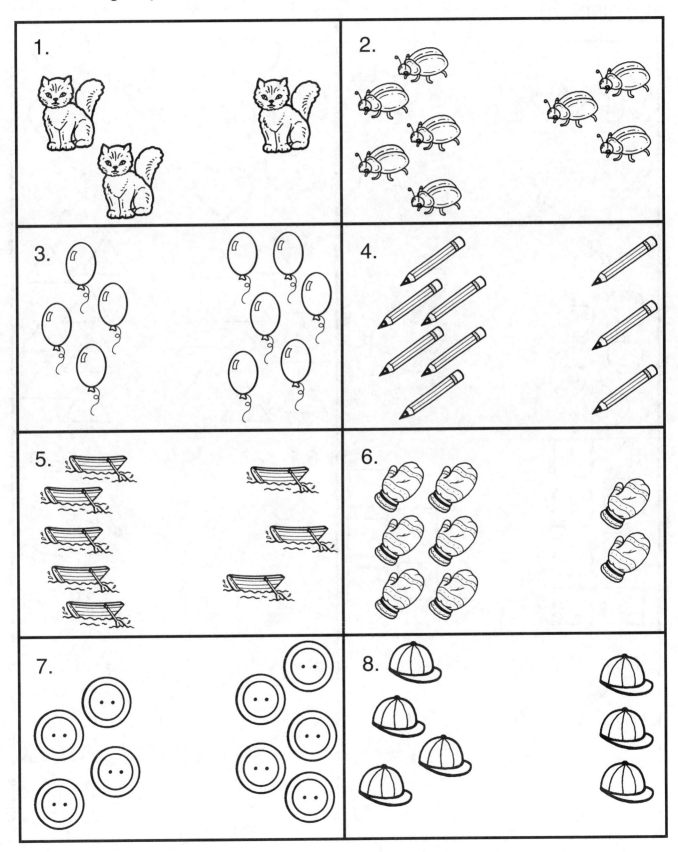

Which Has More?

Circle the group that has more things in it.

1.

2.

3.

4.

5.

6.

7.

8.

Matching Numbers

Draw a line to match the same numbers.

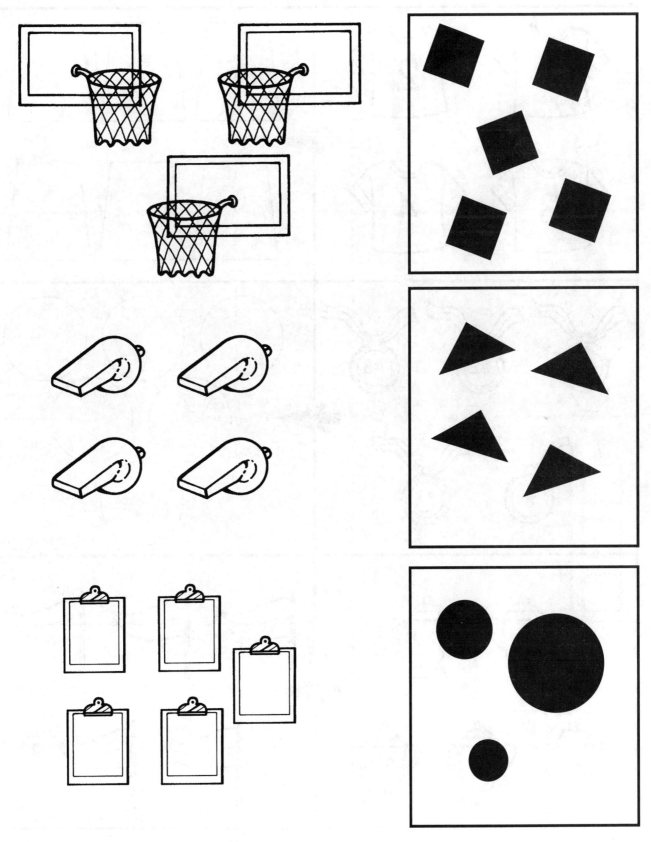

Same Numbers

Color the same number of shapes.

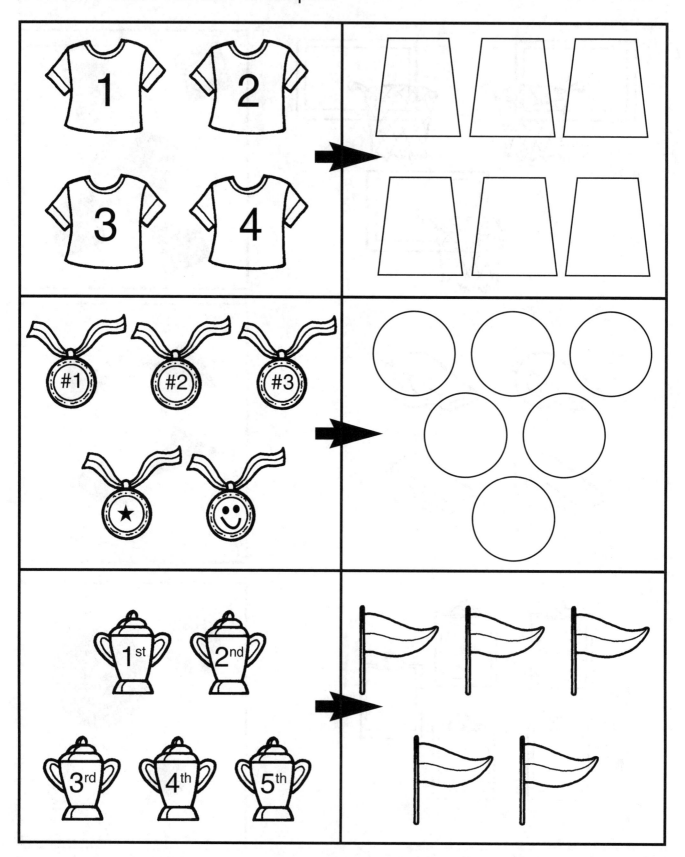

Equal Groups

Draw a line between the groups that have the same number of items in them.

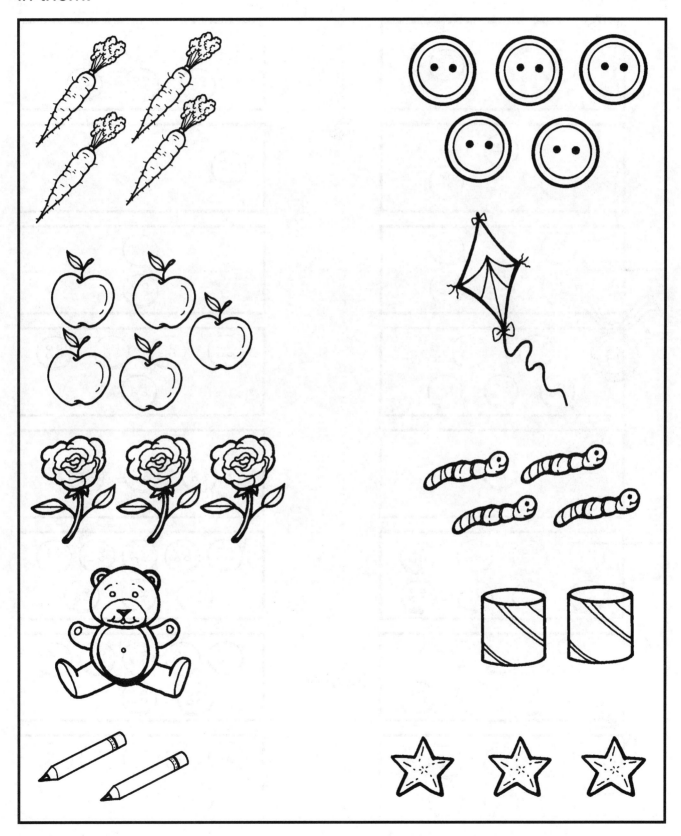

Matching Groups

Match sets that have the same number in them. Draw a line to equal groups.

1.

2.

3.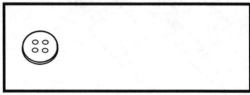

4.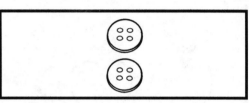

5.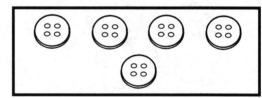

6.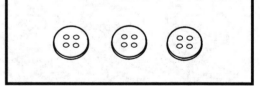

7.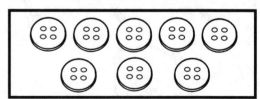

8.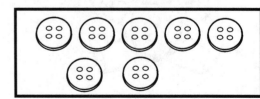

Estimating in the Garden

Estimate how many are in each group. Write your estimate. Then count the items in each group. Write the true number.

1.

Estimate _____

Number _____

2.

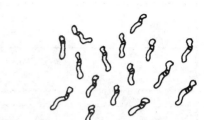

Estimate _____

Number _____

3.

Estimate _____

Number _____

4.

Estimate _____

Number _____

5.

Estimate _____

Number _____

6.

Estimate _____

Number _____

7.

Estimate _____

Number _____

8.

Estimate _____

Number _____

Shortest

Directions: Color the shortest object in each row.

Longest

Directions: Color the longest object in each row.

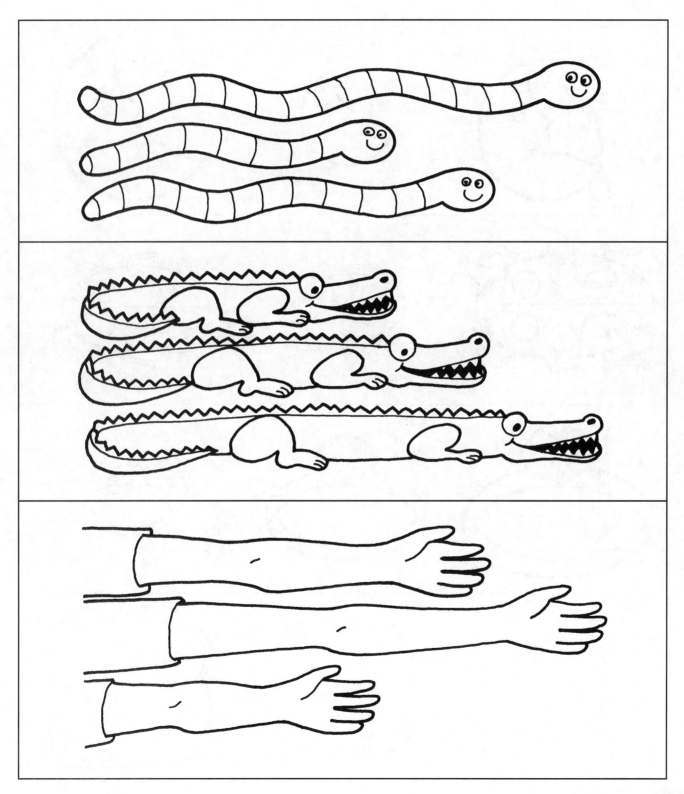

Smallest

Directions: Color the smallest object in each row.

Biggest

Directions: Color the biggest object in each row.

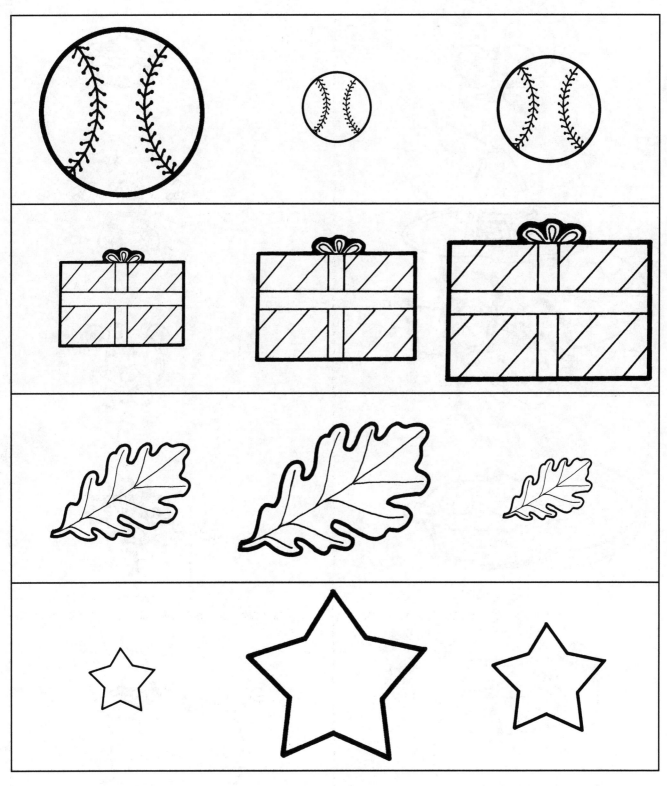

Matching Sizes

Match like big and small pictures. Color.

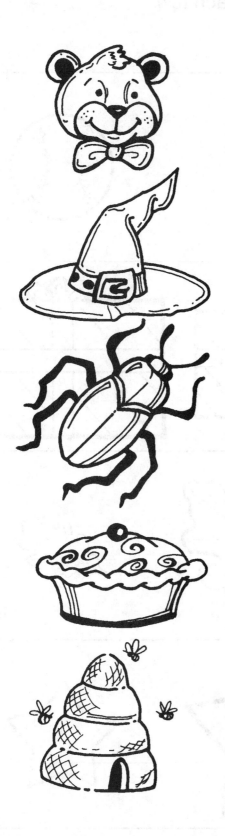

Turkeys

Draw a line to match the turkeys that are the same size.

What Comes Next?

Draw the next thing in each series.

1.

2.

3.

4.

5.

Colorful Beads

Continue each pattern.

Color the beads.

1.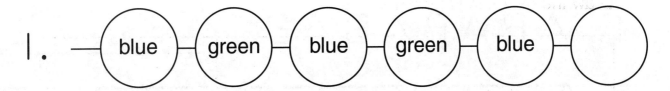

blue — green — blue — green — blue — ( )

2.

orange — purple — orange — purple — orange — ( )

3.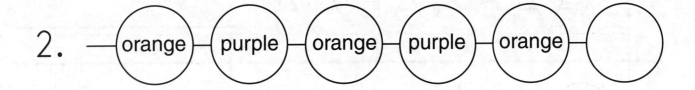

red — red — blue — red — red — ( )

4.

black — white — black — white — ( ) — ( )

5.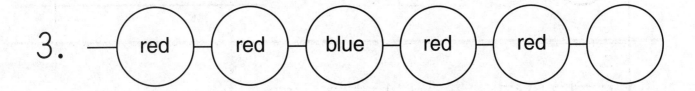

brown — yellow — yellow — brown — yellow — ( )

6.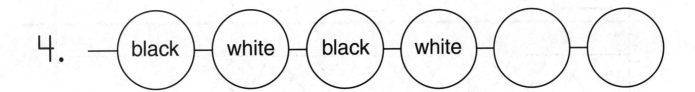

red — blue — blue — red — blue — ( )

Patterns with Letters and Numbers

Write the next letter or number in each series.

1. A B A B A B A B _____

2. A A B A A B A A _____

3. A B B A B B A B _____

4. 1 2 1 2 1 2 1 _____

5. X X X Y X X X Y X X X _____

6. 1 2 2 1 2 2 1 2 _____

7. A B C A B C A B _____

Patterning

Continue each pattern by drawing what comes next.

1. 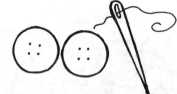 _____ _____ _____

2.  _____ _____ _____

3. 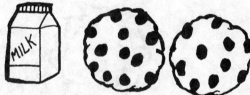 _____ _____ _____

4.  _____ _____ _____

5.  _____ _____

6.  _____ _____ _____

Morning or Evening

Circle the word **morning** or **evening** to tell when you do each activity below.

1.

morning	evening

2.

morning	evening

3.

morning	evening

4.

morning	evening

5.

morning	evening

6.

morning	evening

Day or Night

Draw a picture of something you do during the day. Draw a picture of something you do at night.

Night	**Day**

Time Match

Match each clock to the written time by drawing a line.

1.   **3:00**

2.   **8:00**

3.   **5:00**

4.   **1:00**

5.   **11:00**

6.   **12:00**

Telling Time

Write the correct time under each clock. Use the bank to help you write the time correctly.

Bank					
2:00	10:00	4:00	7:00	6:00	9:00

1.

_____

2.

_____

3.

_____

4.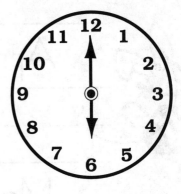

_____

5.

_____

6.

_____

Months of the Year

Write the names of the months on the lines.

January

_____

- - - - - - - - - - - - -

_____

February

_____

- - - - - - - - - - - - -

_____

March

_____

- - - - - - - - - - - - -

_____

April

_____

- - - - - - - - - - - - -

_____

May

_____

- - - - - - - - - - - - -

_____

June

_____

- - - - - - - - - - - - -

_____

July

_____

- - - - - - - - - - - - -

_____

August

_____

- - - - - - - - - - - - -

_____

September

_____

- - - - - - - - - - - - -

_____

October

_____

- - - - - - - - - - - - -

_____

November

_____

- - - - - - - - - - - - -

_____

December

_____

- - - - - - - - - - - - -

_____

Rabbit Hop

Count forward to add. Put the rabbit forward two jumps on each number line. Write the number where he stops.

1.

2 + 2 = _____

| 0 | 1 | 2 | 3 | 4 | 5 | 6 |

2.

1 + 2 = _____

| 0 | 1 | 2 | 3 | 4 | 5 | 6 |

3.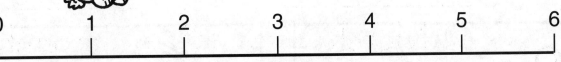

3 + 2 = _____

| 0 | 1 | 2 | 3 | 4 | 5 | 6 |

4.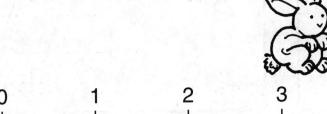

4 + 2 = _____

| 0 | 1 | 2 | 3 | 4 | 5 | 6 |

5.

0 + 2 = _____

| 0 | 1 | 2 | 3 | 4 | 5 | 6 |

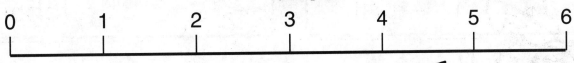

Practice and Learn—Kindergarten

School "Stuff"

Write the sums.

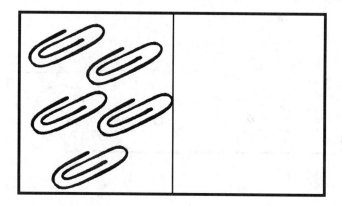

1. 5 + 0 = ____

2. 1 + 3 = ____

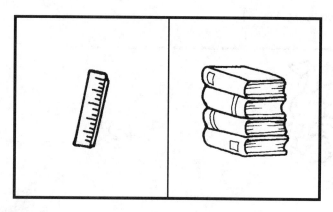

3. 1 + 4 = ____

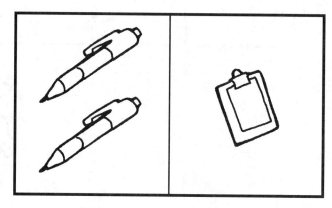

4. 2 + 2 = ____

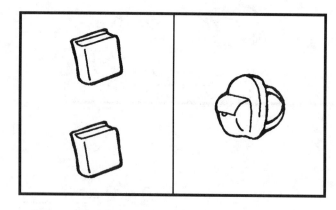

5. 2 + 1 = ____

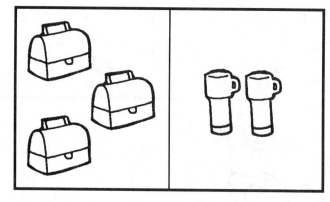

6. 3 + 2 = ____

It's Recess

Write the addition number sentences.

 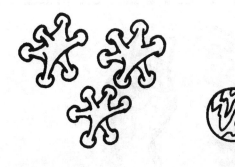

1. $\underline{4}$ + $\underline{1}$ = $\underline{5}$ 2. __ + __ = __

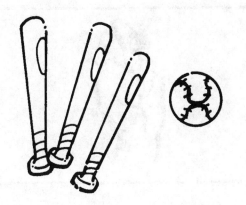 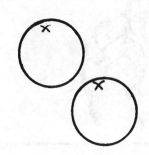

3. __ + __ = __   4. __ + __ = __

5. __ + __ = __

237   *Practice and Learn—Kindergarten*

Everything Counts!

Count the things in each box. Write the number sentence that tells how many in all.

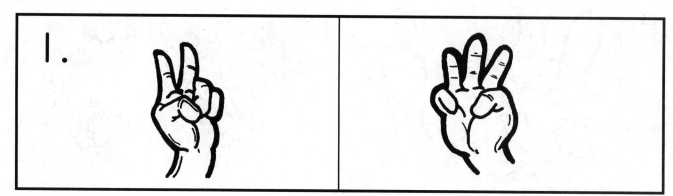

$$\underline{\;2\;} + \underline{\;3\;} = \underline{\;\;\;}$$

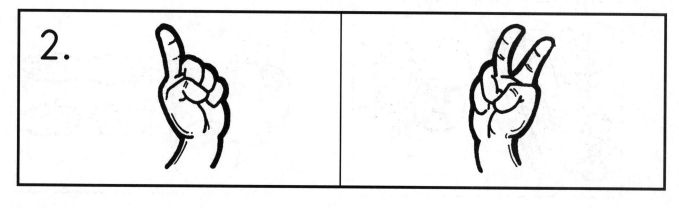

$$\underline{\;\;\;} + \underline{\;\;\;} = \underline{\;\;\;}$$

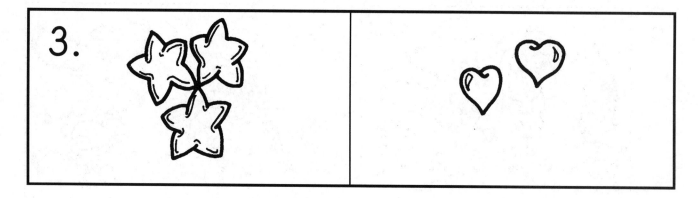

$$\underline{\;\;\;} + \underline{\;\;\;} = \underline{\;\;\;}$$

Add It Up!

Count the things in each box. Write the addition problems.

a.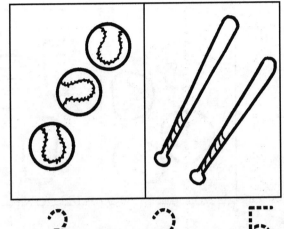

___3___ + ___2___ = ___5___

d.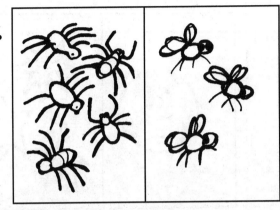

_____ + _____ = _____

b.

_____ + _____ = _____

e.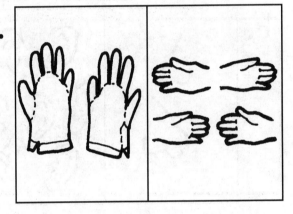

_____ + _____ = _____

c.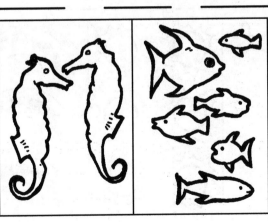

_____ + _____ = _____

f.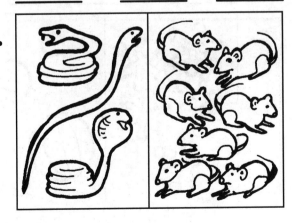

_____ + _____ = _____

More Add It Up!

Count the things in each box. Write the addition problems.

a.

$\underset{\rule{1cm}{0.4pt}}{1} \ + \ \underset{\rule{1cm}{0.4pt}}{3} \ = \ \underline{\hspace{1cm}}$

b.
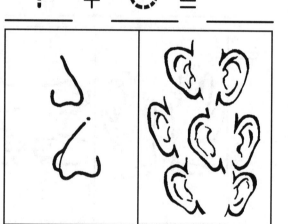

$\underline{\hspace{1cm}} \ + \ \underline{\hspace{1cm}} \ = \ \underline{\hspace{1cm}}$

c.

$\underline{\hspace{1cm}} \ + \ \underline{\hspace{1cm}} \ = \ \underline{\hspace{1cm}}$

d.

$\underline{\hspace{1cm}} \ + \ \underline{\hspace{1cm}} \ = \ \underline{\hspace{1cm}}$

e.

$\underline{\hspace{1cm}} \ + \ \underline{\hspace{1cm}} \ = \ \underline{\hspace{1cm}}$

f.
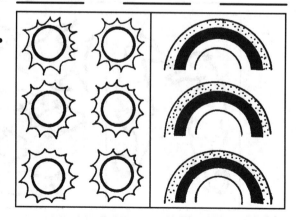

$\underline{\hspace{1cm}} \ + \ \underline{\hspace{1cm}} \ = \ \underline{\hspace{1cm}}$

Addition

Count the things in each box. Write the addition problems.

a.

$\underline{}$ + $\underline{}$ = $\underline{}$

d.

$\underline{}$ + $\underline{}$ = $\underline{}$

b.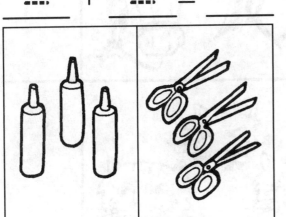

$\underline{}$ + $\underline{}$ = $\underline{}$

e.

$\underline{}$ + $\underline{}$ = $\underline{}$

c.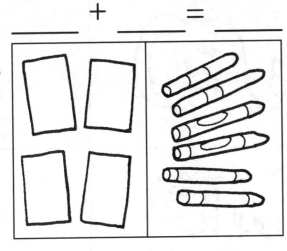

$\underline{}$ + $\underline{}$ = $\underline{}$

f.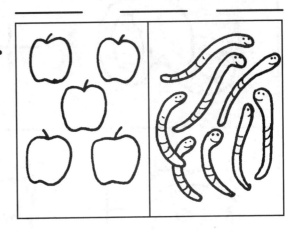

$\underline{}$ + $\underline{}$ = $\underline{}$

Adding One

Write the sums.

1. Example	4
2.	
3.	
4.	
5.	

Bear Puzzle Math

1. Add.

2. Write the numeral.

3. Color using the color code.

4. Cut the pieces out and make a bear.

Color code			
brown	4	yellow	3
blue	2	red	1

Sailboats on the Sea

Write an addition number sentence to go with each set of pictures.

1. _____ + _____ = _____

2. _____ + _____ = _____

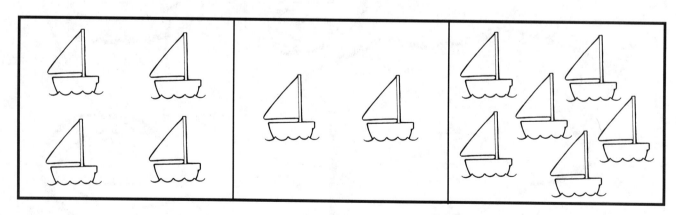

3. _____ + _____ = _____

Sun Catcher

Add.

Color the picture using the key.

Color Key	
4 = yellow	6 = red
7 = orange	12 = purple

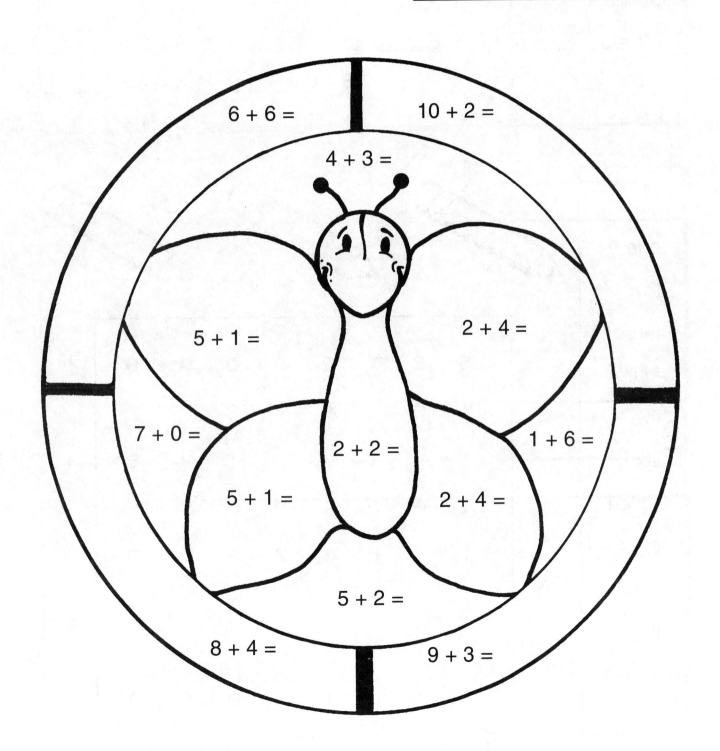

6 + 6 =

10 + 2 =

4 + 3 =

5 + 1 =

2 + 4 =

7 + 0 =

2 + 2 =

1 + 6 =

5 + 1 =

2 + 4 =

5 + 2 =

8 + 4 =

9 + 3 =

Circle the Number Words

Find the sum of the number pairs. Then circle the number words hidden in the letter maze. The words are written across.

Example: 0 + 0 = 0

3 + 2 = _____   8 + 3 = _____   5 + 4 = _____   4 + 3 = _____

2 + 1 = _____   5 + 1 = _____   6 + 6 = _____   6 + 2 = _____

1 + 0 = _____   9 + 1 = _____   1 + 1 = _____   3 + 1 = _____

zero
one
two
three
four
five
six
seven
eight
nine
ten
eleven
twelve

s	e	v	e	n	o	n	e
w	e	l	e	v	e	n	z
l	v	t	w	e	l	v	e
t	e	n	i	n	e	s	i
f	o	u	r	z	e	r	o
e	i	g	h	t	w	o	g
l	f	i	v	e	s	i	x
h	t	h	r	e	e	f	n

Subtraction in Action

| a. Cross out 4 sandwiches. | b. Cross out 2 peanuts. | c. Cross out 1 pineapple. |

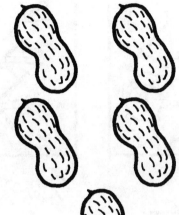

How many are left?_____ | How many are left?_____ | How many are left?_____

| d. Cross out 5 worms. | e. Cross out 3 shells. | f. Cross out 0 clocks. |

How many are left?_____ | How many are left?_____ | How many are left?_____

Practice and Learn—Kindergarten

Wake Up, Sleepyhead!

Write how many are left.

1.   6 – 2 = __

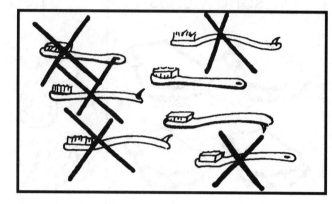

2.   7 – 5 = __

3.   8 – 3 = __

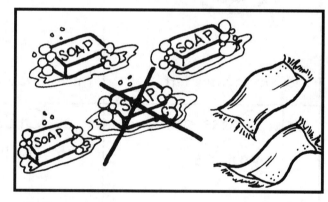

4.   6 – 1 = __

5.   5 – 1 = __

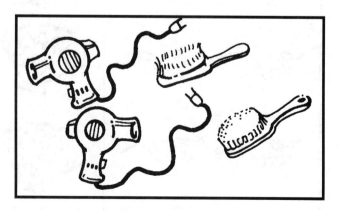

6.   4 – 0 = __

Subtraction

Use the pictures to solve these problems.

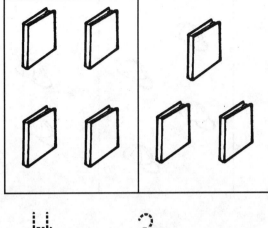   

4 − 3 = ___

___ − ___ = ___

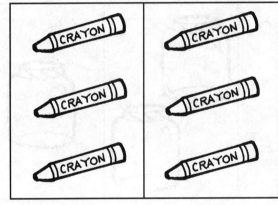   

___ − ___ = ___   ___ − ___ = ___

   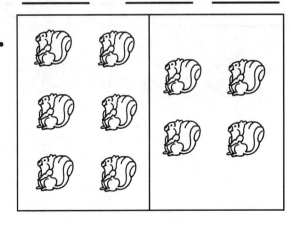

___ − ___ = ___   ___ − ___ = ___

More Subtraction

Use the pictures to solve these problems.

a.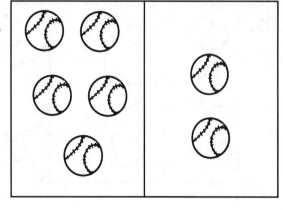

b.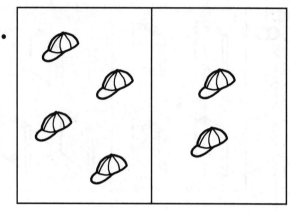

$$5 - 2 = \underline{\hspace{1cm}}$$

$$\underline{\hspace{1cm}} - \underline{\hspace{1cm}} = \underline{\hspace{1cm}}$$

c.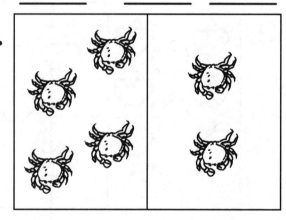

d.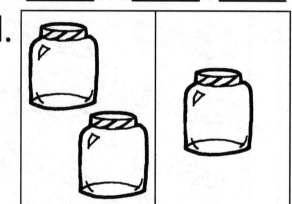

$$\underline{\hspace{1cm}} - \underline{\hspace{1cm}} = \underline{\hspace{1cm}}$$

$$\underline{\hspace{1cm}} - \underline{\hspace{1cm}} = \underline{\hspace{1cm}}$$

e.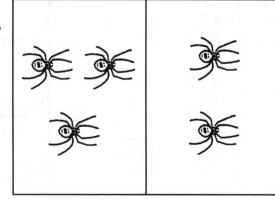

f.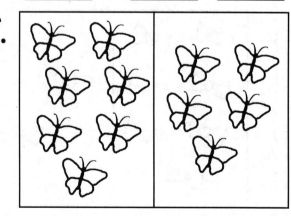

$$\underline{\hspace{1cm}} - \underline{\hspace{1cm}} = \underline{\hspace{1cm}}$$

$$\underline{\hspace{1cm}} - \underline{\hspace{1cm}} = \underline{\hspace{1cm}}$$

Walking a Tightrope

Trace each line with your finger, then a crayon.

Lost Mittens

1. Help each kitten find his mitten.

2. Trace the lines.

3. Color.

Bears and Buttons

Trace the lines from the buttons to the bears.

Write the number of the button on the line below the bear.

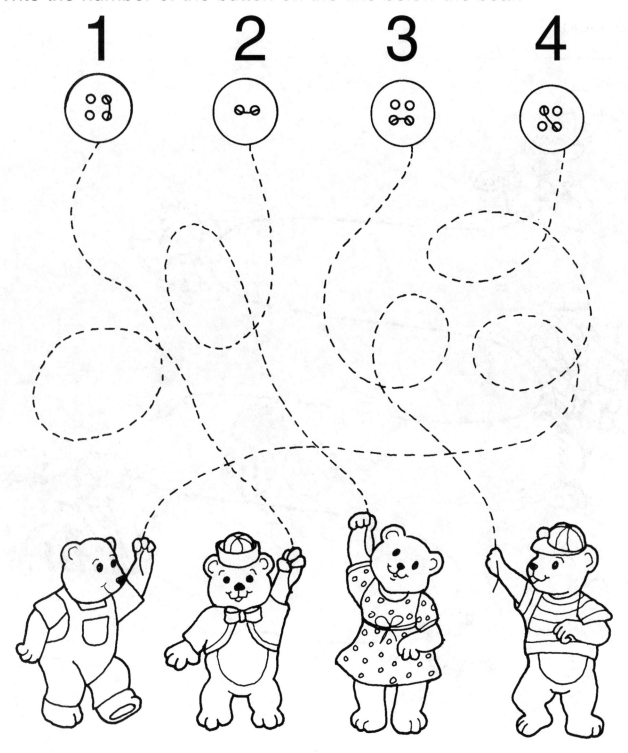

_____   _____   _____   _____

Going to the Circus

Trace the path with your finger, then a crayon.

Maze

Help Officer Flossy catch Dingo Dog!

1. Follow the road with your pencil.

2. Color Goldbug yellow.

3. Color Officer Flossy blue.

4. Color Dingo Dog green.

Officer Flossy

Dingo Dog

Find the Ballerina

Help the soldier find the ballerina.

Color.

Find Your Way Home

Directions: Draw a line to help Poinsettia find her way home. Do not cross any lines.

Matching Parts

Color the first picture in each row. Color the other picture in the row that matches the part to the whole.

Wholes and Parts

Draw a line from the wholes to the parts. Color.

Hooves and Paws

Match the animal faces and feet. Color the pictures.

1.

A.

2.

B.

3.

C.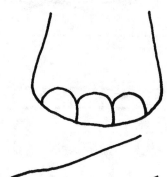

4.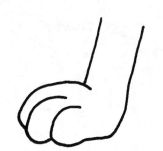

D.

5.

E.

Make It Good As New

1. Fix these by drawing their missing parts.
2. Trace the words.

teddy bear

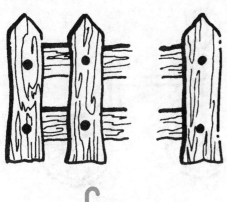

fence

wagon

fire engine

sandbox

swing

What's Missing?

Draw in the missing part of each picture from these things that go.

Car

Wagon

Wheel barrow

Bike

Ice skates

Airplane

Shadows

Draw a line from the object to the shadow.

Color the picture.

Matching Mittens

Draw lines to match each pair of mittens. Color the mittens. Use the same color for each pair.

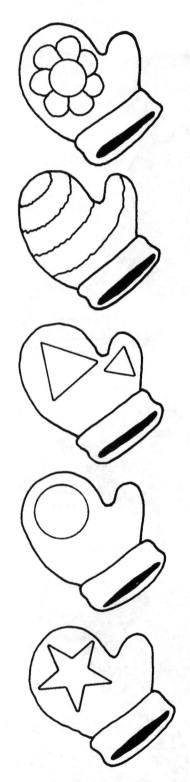

Challenge: Can you draw a matching hat for one pair of mittens?

Clothes Matching

Match the shirt to the hat.

Belonging

Can you tell which children belong to which parents? Color matching
patterns the same color.

Down on My Tummy

Match the like seashells. Color.

Clown Clothes

Color the things a clown would wear.

Circus Act

Name the things in each ring. Then put an X on the one that doesn't belong. Tell why it doesn't belong.

Animals

Color the animals. Name the animals.

All Set?

Circle the things which belong in each set.

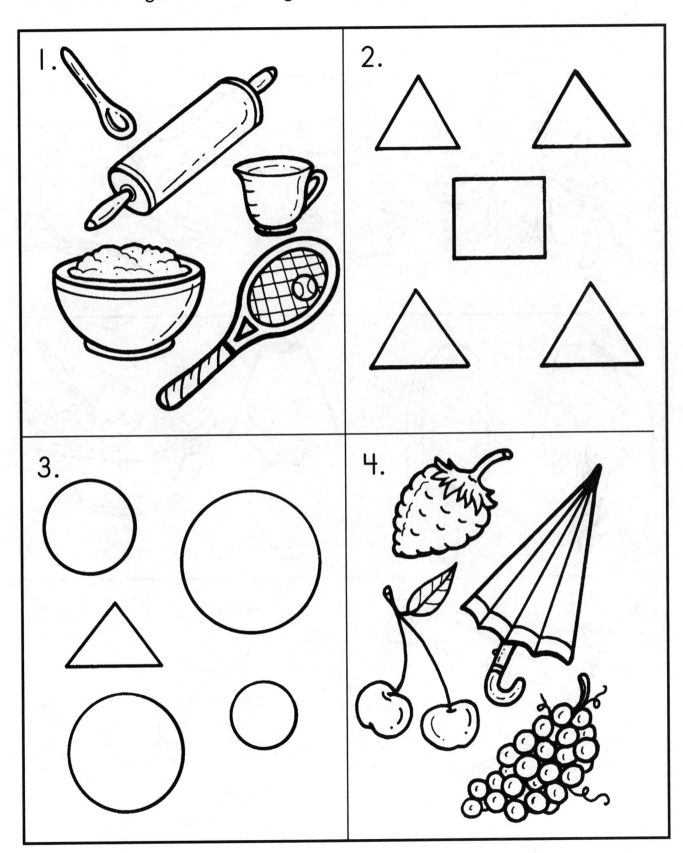

Which Belongs?

Circle things which belong in each set. Cross out things which do not belong.

1.

2.

3.

Go Togethers

Match the things that go together. Draw lines to connect them.

What Goes Together?

Match the things that go together. Color the pictures.

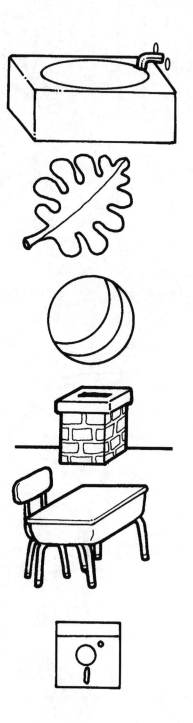

Make a Set

Match the things that go together. Color the pictures.

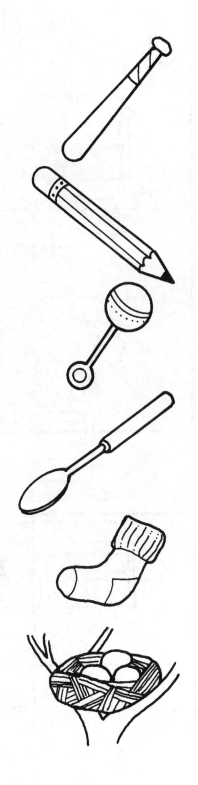

What Am I?

Color, cut, and glue pictures in the correct group.

people	animals
plants	**fish**

What Do We Wear?

Color everything that a person might wear.

Can you find the opposites?

Circle the correct word and color the picture.

1.

big   little

2.

big   little

3.

in   out

4.

in   out

5.

over   under

6.

over   under

7.

on   off

8.

on   off

Find the Opposite

Look at the first picture in each row. Circle the opposites.

Animal Opposites

Draw a line from the picture on the left to the one on the right that shows the opposite.

Opposites

Draw a line to match the opposites.

1. up

2. hot

3. happy

4. day

5. black

6. full

7. young

8. open

sad

white

down

cold

old

night

closed

empty

More Opposites

Draw a line to match the opposites.

1. head

2. big

3. left

4. on

5. laugh

6. fire

7. sit

8. sun

small

cry

foot

under

right

stand

moon

ice

Hidden Hats

1. Find the hidden hats.

2. Circle them and color the picture.

Hide and Go Seek

The teddy bears are playing hide and seek in their room. How many of them can you find? Color them.

Button, Button

How many buttons are in the picture? Color each one you find and count them all. Remember to look for the lost buttons!

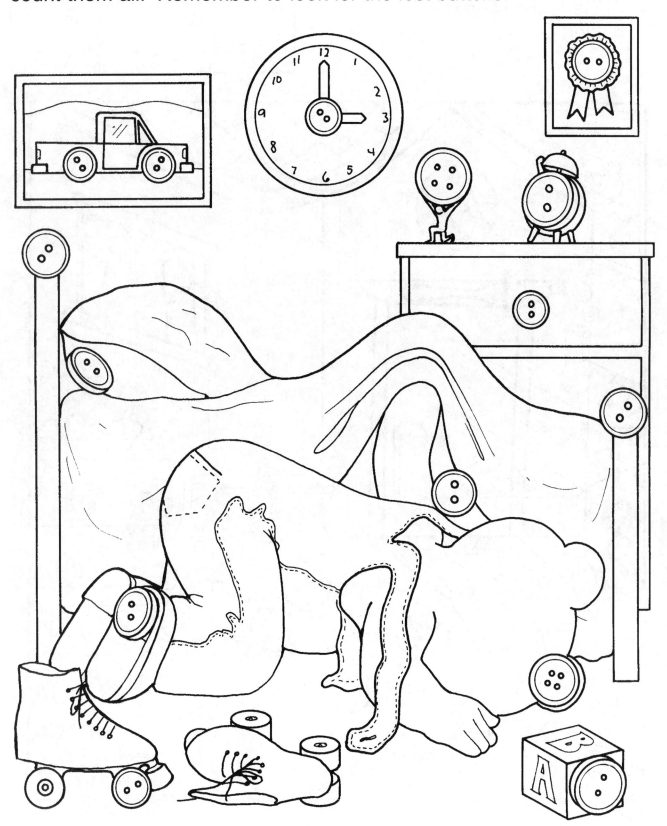

Hidden Pictures

1. Find the hidden pictures.

2. Circle and color the
   hidden pictures.

pail	spoon
T-shirt	shoe
bird	pie

Papa's Pig Pen

1. Read the letter "p" words in the box below.

2. Circle all the letter "p" pictures above.

3. Color the picture.

pencil	penny	picture	pizza
piggy bank	pie	pitcher	

My Own Zoo

1. Read the letter "z" words in the box below.

2. Circle all the letter "z" pictures above.

3. Color the picture.

zigzag	zoo	zebra	zero
zinnia	zipper	zucchini	

Clowning Around

Color the first clown in each row. Color the clown that is the same.

Which Are the Same?

Directions: Color the pictures in each row that are the same.

Musically the Same

Circle the picture that is different from the first picture in each row.
Color the pictures that are the same.

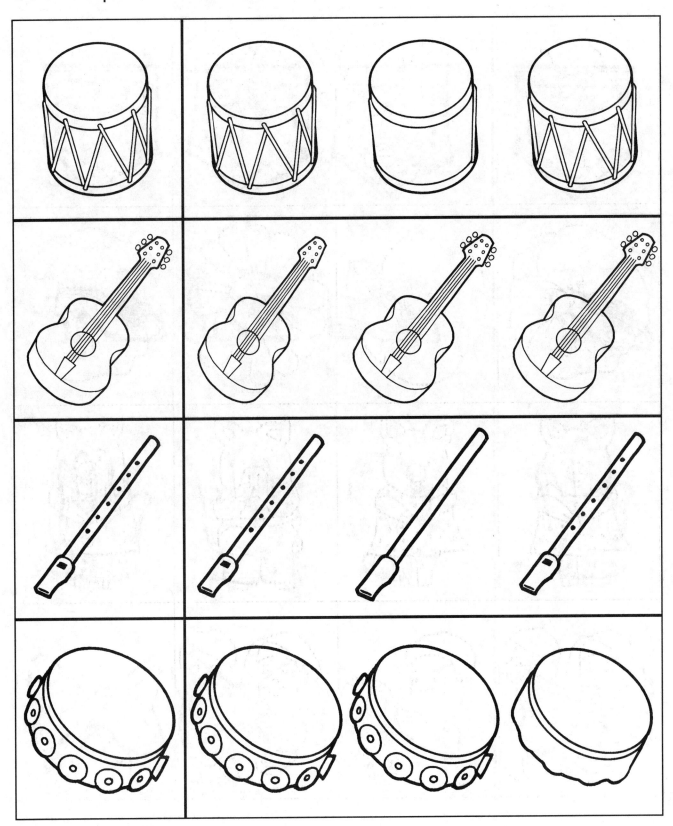

Clothes Match

Look at the first picture in the row. Color the one that is different.

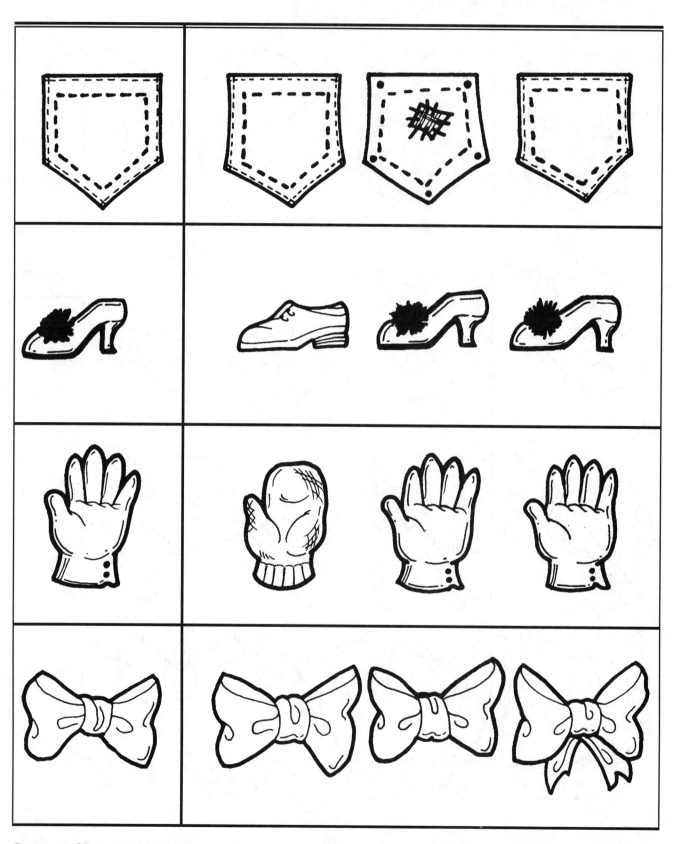

Important Things

1. Color the thing in each row whose number is different.

2. Write the number that is different in the box.

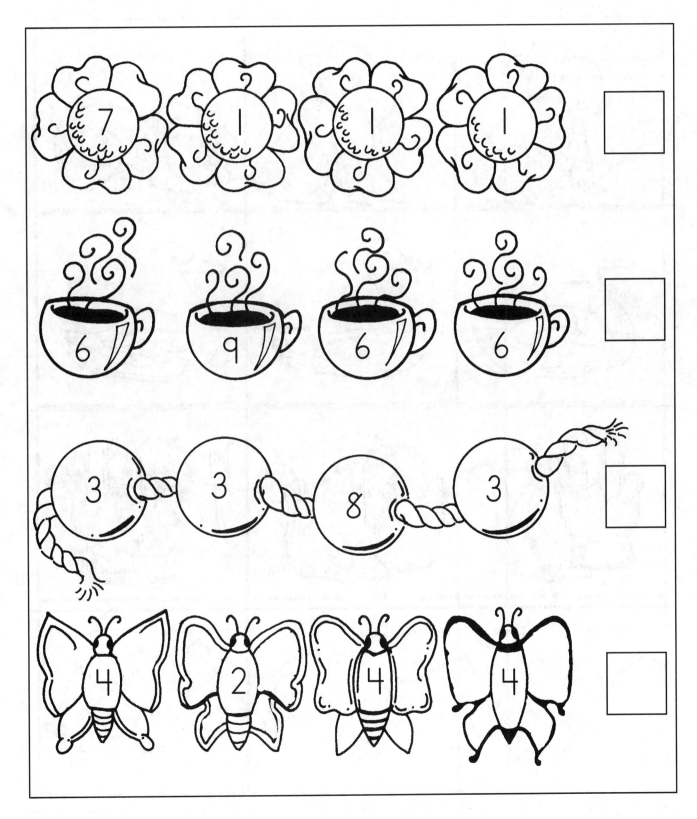

One Is Different

Put an X on the one that is different in each row. Color the ones that are alike.

One Is Different

Put an X on the one that is different in each row. Color the ones that are alike.

Building a Sandcastle

Show the order of the story by writing the numbers 1, 2, 3, and 4 in the correct boxes.

Flying a Kite

Show the order of the story by writing the numbers 1, 2, 3, and 4 in the correct boxes.

Making a Cake

Show the order of the story by writing the numbers 1, 2, 3, and 4 in the correct boxes.

Answer Key

Page 16 What Comes Next?
1. G   8. Z
2. M   9. O
3. S   10. I
4. Y   11. Z
5. H   12. V
6. N   13. P
7. T   14. J

Page 48 Celebrate the Way "A" Sounds
Color: alligator, ant

Page 49 Celebrate the Way "B" Sounds
Color: bear, blimp, bicycle, baseball, bananas, bird, broom, bubbles, bow, bees, bag, bottles, box, bell, bat, bulb, ball, balloons, buttons

Page 50 Celebrate the Way "C" Sounds
Circle: cat, camel, cow, car
Box: centipede, cereal

Page 52 Celebrate the Way "E" Sounds
egg, eagle, elephant

Page 55 Celebrate the Way "H" Sounds
horse, hippopotamus

Page 58 Celebrate the Way "K" Sounds
koala, kite, king, kiss, kitten

Page 59 Celebrate the Way "L" Sounds
lion, letter, ladder, leopard, lollipop

Page 62 Celebrate the Way "O" Sounds
Circle: octopus, octagon, owl, orangutan, orange, ostrich

Page 65 Celebrate the Way "S" Sounds
Circle: sun, snowman, seal, slide, snake, squirrels

Page 69 Celebrate the Way "X" and "Y" Sound
Box: yawn, yarn, yo-yo

Page 70 Celebrate the Way "Z" Sounds
Color: zebra, zipper, zoo, zig-zag

Page 71 Missing Letters
1. a   2. n   3. p
4. v   5. k   6. c
7. f   8. g   9. b

Page 72 More Missing Letters
1. b   2. f   3. r
4. s   5. d   6. f
7. l   8. v   9. c

Page 73 Ending Sounds
1. r   2. m   3. t
4. d   5. g   6. g
7. p   8. n   9. r

Page 74 Ending Sounds
1. p   2. p   3. t
4. k   5. n   6. x
7. t   8. n   9. b

Page 75 Missing Vowels
1. i   2. o   3. o
4. a   5. e   6. u
7. a   8. i   9. a

Page 76 More Missing Vowels
1. a 2. e 3. e 4. i 5. i 6. u 7. u 8. u 9. a

Page 77 Sound It Out
1. top 2. leg 3. six 4. box 5. pen 6. fox 7. star 8. hand 9. flag

Page 78 Sound It Out
1. jar 2. bed 3. ten 4. fan 5. web 6. pin 7. swim 8. drop or tear 9. nest or eggs

Page 79 Match and Rhyme
flag - bag, key - tree, shower - flower, dish - fish, note - boat

Page 80 Rhyme the Pictures
snake - cake, fly - tie, star - jar, heart - cart, clock - sock

Page 81 Find My Rhyming Pair
boat - goat, mouse - house, rain - train, ham - jam, dog - log

Page 82 What Am I?
can - man, fan, ran, let - met, set, get, jet - wet; take - make; hit - sit; mean - bean, seen, lean, clean, dean, queen; mop - top

Page 83 My Fat Cat
sat, mat, bat, rat, hat, fat

Page 84 My Pet, Jet
met, set, jet, let, get, wet

Page 85 Making Rhyming Words
1. cat – hat, bat 2. hog – log, dog 3. man – can, fan
4. pop – mop, top 5. dig – pig, wig 6. ten – pen, hen

Page 87 Above or Below
1. below 2. above 3. below 4. above

Page 88 Left or Right
1. right 2. left 3. left 4. right

Page 89 In or Out
1. in 2. out 3. in 4. out

Page 108 "Little Miss Muffet"
1. curds and whey 2. spider 3. no 4. frightened
5. ran away

Page 116 "Peter, Peter, Pumpkin Eater"
2, 1, 3

Page 121 He Stuck in His Thumb
And pulled out a plum

Page 123 Humpty Dumpty's Fall
4, 2, 1, 3

Answer Key (cont.)

Page 128 "Jack Be Nimble"
jet, jacket, jack o'lantern, jar

Page 129 "Pease Porridge Hot"
Blue: ice cube, ice-cream cone, snowman; Red: soup, sun, candle

Page 197 How Many Berries?
a. 2 b. 2 c. 4 d. 5 e. 6 f. 7

Page 198 How Many?
a. 1 b. 4 c. 2 d. 8 e. 4 f. 9 g. 10 h. 6

Page 199 Count the Library Books
5, 2, 4, 3, 6

Page 200 Count the Objects
1. 5 2. 7 3. 3 4. 6 5. 8 6. 2 7. 4 8. 1

Page 201 How Many Are There?
1. 10 2. 9 3. 9 4. 10 5. 8 6. 7

Page 202 Beach Bears
1 sand castle, 3 birds, 3 bears, 2 pails, 1 ball, 3 boats, 2 shovels, 3 umbrellas, 1 sun, 0 rafts

Page 203 Coloring Fun
1. 6 yellow things 2. 6 red things 3. 6 blue things

Page 204 Number Names
five – 5, three – 3, one – 1, four – 4, two – 2

Page 205 How Many Bees?
15 bees

Page 206 Snowflakes
12 snowflakes

Page 207 Counting People

1. 2	2. 5
3. 8	4. 1
5. 3	6. 4
7. 10	8. 6
9. 7	10. 9

Page 213 Which Has Fewer?

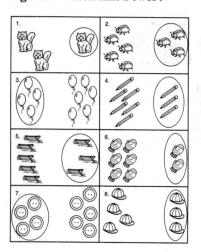

Page 214 Which Has More?

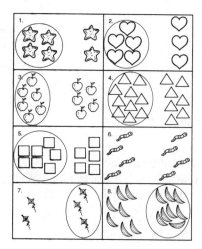

Page 215 Matching Numbers

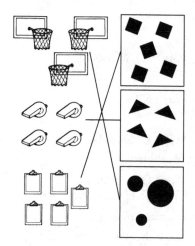

Page 216 Same Numbers

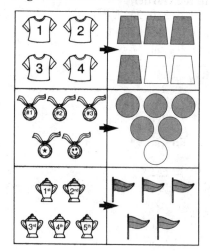

Answer Key (cont.)

Page 217 Equal Groups

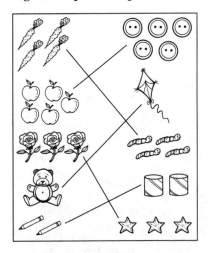

Page 218 Matching Groups

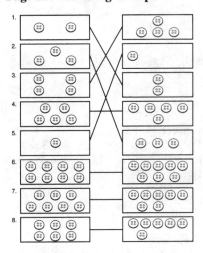

Page 219 Estimating in the Garden

1. 10 2. 16 3. 20 4. 12 5. 5 6. 25 7. 7 8. 1

Page 220 Shortest

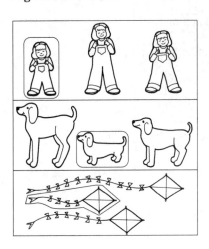

Page 221 Longest

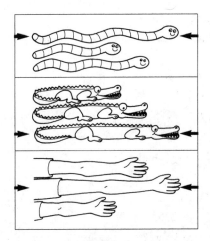

Page 222 Smallest

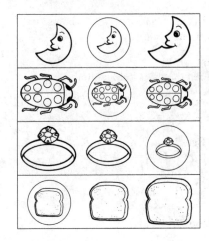

Page 223 Biggest

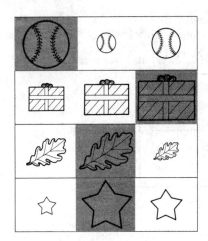

Answer Key (cont.)

Page 224 Matching Sizes

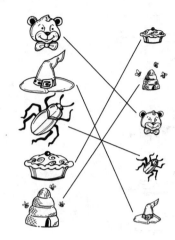

Page 225 Turkeys

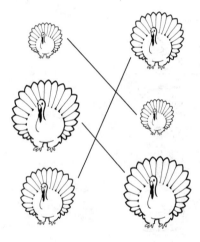

Page 226 What Comes Next?
1. heart 2. triangle 3. heart 4. triangle 5. square

Page 227 Colorful Beads
1. green 2. purple 3. blue 4. black, white 5. yellow 6. blue

Page 228 Patterns with Letters and Numbers
1. A 2. B 3. B 4. 2 5. 6. Y 6. 2 7. C

Page 229 Patterning
1. button, button, needle 2. bee, hive, bee 3. milk, cookie, cookie 4. mitten, mitten, mitten 5. kite, balloon, kite 6. crayon, paper, paper

Page 230 Morning or Evening
1. morning 2. evening 3. morning 4. evening 5. morning 6. evening

Page 232 Time Match
1. 3:00 2. 5:00 3. 8:00 4. 11:00 5. 12:00 6. 1:00

Page 233 Telling Time
1. 7:00 2. 2:00 3. 4:00 4. 6:00 5. 9:00 6. 10:00

Page 235 Rabbit Hop
1. 4 2. 3 3. 5 4. 6 5. 2

Page 236 School "Stuff"
1. 5 2. 4 3. 5 4. 4 5. 3 6. 5

Page 237 It's Recess
1. $4 + 1 = 5$ 2. $3 + 2 = 5$ 3. $3 + 1 = 4$
4. $2 + 0 = 2$ 5. $3 + 2 = 5$

Page 238 Everything Counts
1. $2 + 3 = 5$ 2. $1 + 2 = 3$ $3 + 2 = 5$

Page 239 Add It Up
a. $3 + 2 = 5$ b. $4 + 1 = 5$ c. $2 + 6 = 8$
d. $5 + 3 = 8$ e. $2 + 4 = 6$ f. $3 + 7 = 10$

Page 240 More Add It Up
a. $1 + 3 = 4$ b. $2 + 7 = 9$ c. $5 + 3 = 8$
d. $4 + 3 = 7$ e. $4 + 5 = 9$ f. $6 + 3 = 9$

Page 241 Addition
a. $2 + 2 = 4$ b. $3 + 3 = 6$ c. $4 + 6 = 10$
d. $5 + 1 = 6$ e. $0 + 7 = 7$ f. $5 + 8 = 13$

Page 242 Adding One
1. 4 2. 3 3. 5 4. 2 5. 4

Page 244 Sailboats on the Sea
1. $3 + 2 = 5$
2. $1 + 3 = 4$
3. $4 + 2 = 6$

Page 246 Circle the Number Words
$3 + 2 = 5$ $5 + 3 = 11$ $5 + 4 = 9$ $4 + 3 = 7$
$2 + 1 = 3$ $5 + 1 = 6$ $6 + 6 = 12$ $6 + 2 = 8$
$1 + 0 = 1$ $9 + 1 = 10$ $1 + 1 = 2$ $3 + 1 = 4$

Page 247 Subtraction Action
a. 1 b. 3 c. 3 d. 1 e. 3 f. 5

Page 248 Wake Up, Sleepyhead!
1. 4 2. 2 3. 5 4. 5 5. 4 6. 4

Page 249 Subtraction
a. $4 - 3 = 1$ b. $9 - 5 = 4$ c. $3 - 3 = 0$
d. $10 - 3 = 7$ e. $7 - 2 = 5$ f. $6 - 4 = 2$

Page 250 More Subtraction
a. $5 - 2 = 3$ b. $4 - 2 = 2$ c. $4 - 2 = 2$
d. $2 - 1 = 1$ e. $3 - 2 = 1$ f. $7 - 5 = 2$

Page 260 Hooves and Paws
1. C 2. D 3. E 4. B 5. A

Page 268 Clown Clothes
Color the following: shirt, pants, belt, big shoe, hat

Page 269 Circus Act
Put an X on the following: the shoe, the wagon, the leaf

Page 270 Animals
Color everything in the picture except the man.

Page 271 All Set?
Circle: 1. the spoon, the rolling pin, the measuring cup, the bowl 2. the triangles 3. the circles 4. the strawberries, cherries, grapes

Answer Key (cont.)

Page 272 Which Belongs?
Circle: 1. octopus, fish, whale 2. ice-cream cone, popsicle, sundae 3. screw, saw, hammer, screwdriver, pliers, nail

Page 273 Go Togethers
flower – pot, baby – crib, raincoat – umbrella, crayon – drawing, chair – table, comb – brush

Page 274 What Goes Together?
house – chimney, duck – bathtub, tree – leaf, computer – disk, school – desk, boy – ball

Page 275 Make a Set
fork – spoon, ball – bat, baby – rattle, bird – nest, paper – pencil, shoe – sock

Page 277 What Do We Wear?
Color: hat, shoe, scarf, tie, sock, jacket

Page 278 Can You Find the Opposites?
1. big 2. little 3. in 4. out 5. under 6. over 7. on 8. off

Page 279 Find the Opposite

Page 280 Animal Opposites

Page 281 Opposites

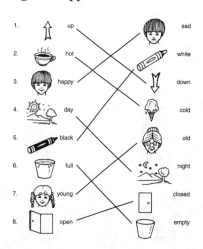

Page 282 More Opposites

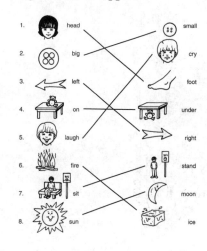

Page 283 Hidden Hats

Practice and Learn—Kindergarten

Answer Key (cont.)

Page 284 Hide and Go Seek

Page 285 Button, Button

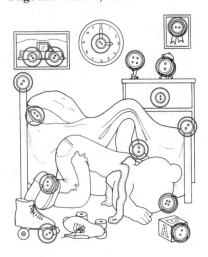

Page 286 Hidden Pictures

Page 287 Papa's Pig Pen

Page 288 My Own Zoo

Page 296 Building a Sandcastle
4, 2, 1, 3

Page 297 Flying a Kite
3, 2, 4, 1

Page 298 Making a Cake
3, 1, 4, 2